Journey to the Cross

✛

Journey to the Cross

✛

Lenten Reflections for Individuals and Groups

MYRA B. NAGEL

WIPF & STOCK · Eugene, Oregon

Wipf and Stock Publishers
199 W 8th Ave, Suite 3
Eugene, OR 97401

Journey to the Cross
Lenten Reflections for Individuals and Groups
By Nagel, Myra B.
Copyright©1996 Pilgrim Press
ISBN 13: 978-1-60608-583-7
Publication date 4/6/2009
Previously published by United Church Press, 1996

Contents

How to Use This Book

The season of Lent is a time for storytelling. It is a time the church has set aside to focus on the stories that stand at the center of the gospel message. We have heard these stories many times, so many times that they may have lost their impact. We may not hear their radical nature; we may gloss over their life-changing news as if it were commonplace.

During this Lenten season, I invite you to try to hear the old, old stories with new ears. I encourage you to listen to each story as if you were hearing it for the first time, to enter the story, to walk to Jerusalem, to stand at the foot of the cross, and to behold the empty tomb.

In this book, I have chosen seven stories that are close to the heart of the gospel. You will find one chapter for each week of Lent if you choose to read the book in that way. If you want to use the book as a guide for daily meditation, you might do it as follows: On the first day, read the section "Coming to the Story" and read the biblical story itself. On the second day, read the section "Reflecting on the Story." For the third, fourth, fifth, and sixth days, focus each day on one or two of the questions and exercises in the section "Living the Story" at the end of each chapter. On the seventh day, do the meditation suggested at the end of "Living the Story."

Storytelling can be even more effective in a group. Why not gather some friends to read and reflect on these stories with you during this Lenten season? You will find a "Guide for Group Study" at the back of the book.

1

"Teacher, Let Me See!"

Coming to the Story

1. What words come to your mind when you think about the season of Lent? Make a list of these words. Underline the words on your list that express feelings. Add some more "feeling" words to your list.
2. Read Mark 8:22–35 and 10:32–52.
3. Which of these stories do you like best? Where do you see yourself in that story?

Reflecting on the Story

Imagine walking into a church and finding a golden gallows above the altar! Or suppose you saw a bronze model of the electric chair. What would you think?

The symbol that hangs over the altar of most Christian churches is a replica of a means of execution. Yet that symbol doesn't startle us. We are used to seeing a cross. Fashioned of gold, silver, or finely crafted wood, the cross hangs in our churches. It dangles from key chains. It adorns our necklaces. We have come to regard it as a thing of beauty. It proclaims victory, joy, and life. We may tend to forget that the cross is also a symbol of sacrifice, suffering, and death.

The season of Lent is a time to reflect on the cross and its meaning for our lives. It is a time to appreciate the joy and also to re-

1

member the sacrifice. It is a time to ask serious questions. Who is Jesus? Is he the Messiah, the Christ? What does it mean to be the Christ? What does it mean to be followers of God's Messiah? What is the place of the cross in our personal faith?

One of the ways to approach these questions is to walk the path that Jesus walked as he journeyed toward the cross, to retell the most significant stories, and to reflect on their meaning for our lives. Many churches have moved away from this pattern of reflecting on the journey to the cross during the season of Lent. Many pastors take the biblical text for their sermons from the *Common Lectionary*, a list of scripture readings that was published by an ecumenical Consultation on Common Texts in 1983.[1] When the members of the consultation chose the lectionary texts for Lent, they reasoned that since the church has always considered every Sunday to be "a little Easter," and Sundays are not counted in the forty days of Lent, the scripture readings for the Sundays of Lent should reflect a quality of "little Easter."[2]

If your pastor follows the lectionary, during Lent you can expect to hear stories of Jesus' temptation in the wilderness, his transfiguration, his cleansing of the temple, his parable of the prodigal son, his raising of Lazarus from death, and his triumphal entry into Jerusalem on Palm Sunday. Unless you go to church on Maundy Thursday or Good Friday, you may not hear the stories of Jesus' journey to the cross.

Yet the journey to the cross is an essential part of the Easter story. Reflecting on the cross and the events that led to it is crucial to Easter faith. During this season of Lent, I invite you to embark on a journey to Jerusalem—and beyond—following in the steps of Jesus. To act as our guide along our way, I have chosen the Gospel of Mark. My selection is admittedly an arbitrary choice. Matthew, Luke, John, and the apostle Paul would also be qualified candidates. But Mark is my own personal favorite; it is the book to which I turn most frequently when I reflect on the cross and its meaning for my own faith. I invite you to set out on a journey with me, with Mark as our guide. Are you ready? Let's be on our way.

A Two-Stage Healing

We begin our journey in Mark, chapter 8, at a village called Bethsaida, which was probably located at the northern tip of the Sea of Galilee. Up to this point, Mark has presented Jesus as a highly popular healer and worker of miracles. In the preceding scene, Jesus had miraculously fed a crowd of five thousand with seven loaves of bread and a few small fish. Now Jesus and the disciples have come to Bethsaida. Some people brought a blind man and begged Jesus to touch him. Jesus took the man by the hand, put saliva on his eyes, and laid hands on him. Then he asked him, "Can you see anything?" The man looked up and said, "I can see people, but they look like trees walking."

In all the Gospel stories, this is the only time Jesus failed to heal completely. The man now could see, but his vision was distorted. Jesus had to touch his eyes a second time before the man's sight was restored and he saw everything clearly (8:22–25).

Distorted Vision

Immediately after this story of a two-stage healing, Mark leads us north to the district of Caesarea Philippi, an area that is now in the Golan Heights. Here, Jesus asked his disciples, "Who do people say that I am?" The disciples answered that some said "John the Baptist, and others, Elijah, and still others, one of the prophets." Then Jesus asked Peter a direct question. "Who do you say that I am?" (8:27–29).

This is the question Mark has been asking his readers in the first eight chapters. Mark has shown us that Jesus taught with authority; he had the power to forgive sin; he healed the sick; he performed miracles; he even had command over nature and made the storm and sea obey. All these events had caused people to wonder, "Who is this Jesus? Could he be the expected Christ?" *Christ* is the Greek form of the Hebrew title *Messiah*, which means "the anointed one." The Jewish people had long expected the coming of a Messiah, a leader anointed by God who would assume the throne of King David and restore the nation to the glory it had known under David's reign. Could Jesus be this Messiah? Jesus put the question to Peter, and to the reader as well. "Who do you say that I am?"

Peter answered, "You are the Messiah."

Jesus' response puzzles us. He sternly ordered the disciples not to tell anyone about him. Then he began to teach them that he must suffer, be rejected and killed, and after three days rise again. Peter didn't like the sound of that! He rebuked Jesus! In reply, Jesus scolded Peter in some of the harshest words in all the Gospel stories: "Get thee behind me, Satan! For you are setting your mind not on divine things, but on human things" (v. 33). The severity of Jesus' response catches us by surprise.

Mark's account of the conversation that took place at Caesarea Philippi is dramatically different from Matthew's. (Keep in mind that the Gospel stories were told aloud for some time before they were written; thus we find differences in the way the stories were remembered and recorded.) In Matthew, Jesus asked Peter the same question, "Who do you say that I am?" Peter answered, "You are the Christ, the son of the living God." Jesus congratulated Peter for his answer. "Blessed are you Simon, son of Jonah," he said. "For flesh and blood has not revealed this to you . . . and I tell you, you are Peter, and on this rock I will build my church" (Matt. 16:13–18). I suspect that for most of us, Matthew's version of this story is the one we prefer. We expect Jesus to affirm Peter's insight, "You are the Christ." Yet in Mark's account, Jesus does not do this. Why not?

We can understand Jesus' response better if we interpret it in the light of the two-stage healing story that preceded it.[3] Jesus had asked the blind man of Bethsaida, "Can you see anything?" At Caesarea Philippi, Jesus asked Peter, "Who do you say that I am?" Mark draws a symbolic connection between the two questions. Jesus is asking Peter, "Can you see the truth about me?" The symbolic connection continues in their answers. The blind man answered, "I can see people, but they look like trees walking." He could see something, but his vision was distorted. Peter could also see something. He could see part of the truth about Jesus. He answered, "You are the Christ." Peter had answered correctly with his lips, but Jesus knew that Peter's vision was still impaired. He had a distorted concept of what it meant to be the Messiah, the Christ. To see the Messiah merely as a healer and worker of miracles was distorted vision. To see the Christ as the fulfillment of the popular expectation of a political leader who would restore the nation of Israel to its former glory was distorted vision.

The disciples—and Mark's readers also—needed a second healing touch in order to see clearly. And so Jesus began to heal the disciples of their blindness. He said, "The Messiah must undergo great suffering and be rejected . . . and be killed and after three days rise again. . . . If any want to become my followers, let them deny themselves, and take up their cross, and follow me. For those who want to save their life will lose it, and those who lose their life for my sake and for the sake of the gospel, will save it" (8:31–35). To try to understand the Messiah, the Christ, outside the context of the cross is distorted vision.

A Crossless Life?

Peter couldn't believe that Jesus had to suffer and die. And Peter was right about one thing: Jesus had other choices. He did not have to embark on a course that led to suffering and death on a cross.

He could have returned to Galilee. Early in his ministry, Jesus had concentrated on the region around Galilee where he had attracted huge crowds and won popular acclaim. He had also made enemies. He had repeatedly criticized the scribes and Pharisees, Judaism's authorities, for their hypocrisy, hard-heartedness, and preoccupation with ritual purity. He accused them of following the letter of the law but forgetting the purpose of the law, which he summed up in the twin commandments of loving God and loving neighbor. The religious authorities were annoyed, but at this point Jesus was more irritating than dangerous to them. If Jesus had remained in the area of Galilee, he probably would not have posed enough threat to the power of the Jewish authorities to warrant putting him to death.

At Caesarea Philippi, where Jesus and his disciples talked together in the foothills of Mount Hermon, Jesus was at a point of decision. He could look south to the way that led back to Galilee. In his mind's eye, he could also look beyond to Jerusalem. Jesus had several options. He could remain silent. He could placate the religious authorities with compromise and soothing words. He could remain in the relative safety of Galilee. Or he could continue southward toward Jerusalem, boldly proclaiming the gospel along the way.

Jerusalem was the home of the Jewish temple, the holy place and center of religious life for the whole nation. It was also the administrative seat of government, from which Herod ruled the region on behalf of the emperor of Rome. Jesus knew that going to Jerusalem would put him on a collision course with the Jewish and Roman authorities. It was a decision that almost inevitably would end in his death.

But God's way led to Jerusalem. If Jesus wanted to proclaim the coming of God's reign in the place where it would make the greatest impact on the most people, he could not avoid Jerusalem. Peter would have taken an easier road. He rebuked Jesus for choosing such a painful path. But Jesus chastised him: "You are setting your mind not on divine things but on human things."

How human it is to want to avoid the path that leads to suffering, cost, rejection, and pain! How human it is to want to lead a crossless life! How human it is to believe that we can experience the joy without the suffering, the victory without the sacrifice. When we are confronted with difficult choices, how human it is to want to take the easy road, as shown in the following examples.

- A business executive discovers that her company is cutting cost by dumping toxic waste into a nearby water supply.
- A political candidate is offered a large contribution to his campaign with the unspoken understanding that if he is elected, he will vote for policies that are favorable to his contributor's corporation.
- A doctor has made a serious error that resulted in injury to a patient. She knows that admitting her mistake and attempting

to make restitution will damage her reputation and hurt her career.

- A soldier on the battlefield spots a grenade about to explode. He can run and save his life, or he can throw himself on the grenade and save the lives of his friends.
- A young man wants to become a concert pianist, but the road ahead involves years of practicing eight hours a day and offers no guarantee of success.
- A wife wants to contribute to a charity whose work she strongly believes in. Her husband is dead set against it.
- A gay person struggles to decide whether or not to come out of the closet.
- A girl is shunned by her high school clique for choosing a friend who is "funny-looking."
- An eighth-grade boy is teased by his friends for refusing to try drugs.
- A married person struggles with the question of whether to end an affair.
- A successful businessman begins to recognize his increasing dependence on alcohol.
- A young woman enters psychiatric treatment and with the help of a competent therapist uncovers, bit by bit, painful memories of her past. At times she thinks she cannot continue to face the anguish, yet she knows it is the only course to wellness.

Indeed, how human it is to want to avoid the path that leads to suffering, cost, rejection, and pain! Much of what I do as a counselor is to help people face the parts of themselves and their lives that they have found too painful to confront. I admit that I am not always able to practice what I teach. I, too, have needed the help of a counselor to recognize my own tendency to avoid conflict and pain.

We can understand how Peter felt when he rebuked Jesus for choosing the path of suffering, rejection, and death. Jesus' answer to Peter might also be directed to us: "You are setting your mind not on divine things but on human things." How human it is to look for an easy way! How human it is to want to lead a crossless life!

Jesus chose the path that led to Jerusalem. Along the way, he continued to correct his followers' distorted vision. He "set their mind on divine things," teaching them the true meaning of discipleship (Mark 8:22–10:52). Twice more, the pattern that we saw at Caesarea Philippi would be repeated: Jesus' prediction of the cross; the disciples' misunderstanding; and Jesus' teaching about the cost of discipleship.

As they passed through Galilee, traveling south along the valley of the Jordan River, Jesus told the disciples that he would be betrayed into human hands and be killed and three days later rise again. The disciples displayed their misunderstanding by arguing about who was the greatest. Jesus taught them, "Whoever wants to be first must be last of all and servant of all" (9:30–37).

They continued southward. They were on their way to Jerusalem, both geographically and symbolically. In the region of Judea, Jesus told his disciples that he would be handed over to the chief priests and scribes, condemned to death, spit upon, flogged, and killed. After three days he would rise again. James and John revealed their misunderstanding by asking Jesus to do them a special favor. Jesus asked them, "What is it that you want me to do for you?" James and John replied, "Grant us to sit one at your right hand and one at your left, in your glory." Jesus asked if they were able to follow him in the way of suffering. "Are you able to drink the cup that I drink or be baptized with the baptism that I am baptized with?" With total lack of comprehension they replied, "We are able." Jesus said to them, "The cup that I drink you will drink and with the baptism with which I am baptized, you will be baptized" (10:32–40).

To follow Christ is to walk in the way of sacrifice, pain, and cost. Jesus said, "Whoever wishes to become great among you must be your servant, and whoever wishes to be first among you must be slave of all" (10:43–44).

Sight Restored

Mark concludes the section on discipleship with a story of the healing of another blind person. Like the two-stage healing that introduced the section, this story of the restoration of sight has a symbolic connection to the stories of the disciples' distorted vision and Jesus' corrective teaching.

On their way to Jerusalem, Jesus and the disciples came to Jericho. As they were leaving, they saw a large crowd. In the midst of this crowd, a blind beggar named Bartimaeus was sitting by the roadside. When he heard that Jesus of Nazareth was approaching, he began to shout out, "Jesus, Son of David, have mercy on me." The people around him told him to be quiet, but he responded by crying even louder, "Son of David, have mercy on me!" (10:46–48).

"Son of David" was another common designation for the Messiah. The Jewish people expected the coming of a leader like David, a "son" of David, who would restore Israel to the glory it had known during David's reign. The blind beggar's recognition of Jesus as "Son of David" echoes Peter's words to Jesus, "You are the Christ."

Jesus heard the beggar's cries and said, "Call him here." The people brought Bartimaeus to him. Jesus asked him, "What do you want me to do for you?" It is the same question Jesus had just asked James and John when they requested a special favor from him. James and John had asked to sit on Jesus' right and left hand in his glory! But Bartimaeus said, "My teacher, let me see again!" This time the healing required no second touch. Jesus said to him, "Go. Your faith has made you well" (10:49–52). Bartimaeus regained his sight and followed Jesus "on the way."

Although the disciples did not yet see clearly, Mark's readers do. We understand that "the way" is the way of discipleship, the way to Jerusalem, the way that must endure the cross before it leads to the victory that lies beyond.

In the next chapters, we will continue to walk with Jesus and his followers on the way to Jerusalem, letting Jesus teach us, not only by his words, but with his life. We will take our questions along with us as we go. Who is Jesus? Is he the Christ? What does it mean to be the Christ? What does it mean to be followers of God's Messiah?

We will notice the disciples' failures to perceive the truth that was in front of their eyes. The disciples will not gain 20/20 vision until Jesus has completed the journey he described to them, the way to Jerusalem and the cross, and finally to the Resurrection beyond.

No doubt we will also discover some distortions in our own vision as Jesus teaches us with his life. As we journey with Jesus "on the way" to the cross, we will ask, like Bartimaeus, "Teacher, let me see."

Living the Story

1. Suppose Jesus said to you, *"(Your name),* who do you say that I am?" How would you answer?
2. Jesus said to Bartimaeus, the blind man, "What do you want me to do for you?" Close your eyes and imagine yourself with Jesus. Choose any setting you wish and picture it in your mind. Then imagine Jesus looking at you and saying, "What do you want me to do for you?" How do you answer?
3. "Reflecting on the Story" suggested that our human tendency is to want to lead a "crossless life." How do you react to that suggestion?
4. What gave Jesus the strength to choose the way that led to Jerusalem and the cross?
5. "Reflecting on the Story" gave examples of some of the hard choices that persons are sometimes called to make. If you can, recall a time when you chose the hard way rather than taking a road that seemed easier. What gave you the strength to choose that way? How might your life and the lives of others have been changed if you had chosen a different road?
6. What hard choice do you see in your life right now? What might Jesus say to you about this choice?
7. What hard choices are now facing your congregation? Your community? Our nation? What might Jesus say about these decisions?
8. Meditate on this line from Psalm 18:30: "God's way is perfect."

This Week

Pray daily the words of Psalm 86:11:

Teach me your way, O God,
that I may walk in your truth;
give me an undivided heart to revere your name.

2

"She Has Done What She Could"

Coming to the Story

1. Recall a costly gift you have received. Don't limit your thinking to money. The cost might be in time, in effort, or in pride. How did receiving this gift make you feel?
2. Read the story about a costly gift in Mark 14:3–9.
3. Where do you see yourself in this story?

Reflecting on the Story

We begin our journey toward the cross about two miles east of Jerusalem at Bethany. The time is two days before the Jewish Feast of the Passover. The setting is the home of Simon, a leper or former leper. Visualize the scene as Mark describes it. Jesus is sharing a meal with some of his followers. Picture yourself among this group of followers.

A woman enters, carrying a long-necked alabaster flask. She attracts your attention immediately. Moving with assurance and a sense of purpose, she makes her way directly to Jesus. Lovingly, she pours something on Jesus' head. Instantly, the room is filled with an exotic aroma. You recognize the scent; it is nard, a very expensive perfumed ointment. Someone on your right mutters, "That ointment must have cost three hundred denarii." A denarius was the typical wage for a day's labor, so the nard was worth a whole year's wages. You turn and look at the speaker. What is your reaction to these words?

The crowd around you begins to murmur, and someone on your left says indignantly, "This ointment could have been sold and the money given to the poor." What do you respond to that comment?

Jesus commands, "Let her alone! Why do you trouble her?" Are you surprised by the sharpness of his tone? Jesus gives the woman a smile of approval, then looks back to his followers who have criticized her. "She has performed a good service to me," he says.

These are some of the highest words of praise that come from the lips of Jesus in all of the Gospel stories. "Good service" here is the Greek *kalos*. Also translated "beautiful," it is the word Jesus used when he spoke of "good fruit," "good seed," and the "good shepherd." Perhaps Jesus senses that you are surprised by the extravagance of his praise. He says, "You always have the poor with you, and you can show kindness to them whenever you wish; but you will not always have me. She has done what she could. She has anointed my body beforehand for its burial. Truly I tell you, wherever the good news is proclaimed in the whole world, what she has done will be told in remembrance of her" (Mark 14:3–9).

Mark's story is brief, and it leaves much to our imagination. Who was this "Simon the leper" whom Jesus chose to visit? We don't know. Who were the others at the meal? In Matthew's account, they were disciples. John's version names the woman's critic as Judas, and he places the incident at the home of Lazarus, Mary, and Martha (12:1–8). Mark simply says, there were "some" who were present. Since they shared a meal with Jesus in Simon's home, they probably were disciples, although not necessarily limited to the Twelve.

Who was the woman, the central figure of the story? Some interpreters have connected her with Luke's account of the woman who bathed Jesus' feet with her tears, the woman whose "sins which were many have been forgiven" (7:36–50). Most scholars, however, think these were two separate incidents. John identifies the woman as Mary. But Mark simply says, "a woman." We don't know who she is.

Mark's focus was not on the *who* of the story; his emphasis was on what happened. The woman's action, the criticism of those who watched, Jesus' reaction—these carry the weight of the story for Mark.

Although this incident is brief, it is important. It sets the scene for the events that follow. At one level, it is a preparation for the cross. In the scene that preceded it, the chief priests and scribes were preparing for the cross by plotting the arrest of Jesus. At Bethany, the preparations were entirely different. A woman anointed Jesus' head with perfumed ointment, and Jesus interpreted her action as anointing his body for its burial. From this point on, the events will move swiftly toward the Crucifixion.

At another level, this story highlights the contrast between the disciples' blindness to the way of the cross and the woman's clear understanding of that way. In the stories we will read as we draw nearer to the Mount of Calvary, the disciples' blindness will grow worse. But in this story, one of Jesus' followers embodies a true understanding of discipleship. This figure is an unnamed woman.

The Blindness of Legalism

Like many of Jesus' teachings, the words of Jesus in this story catch us by surprise. He sharply corrected his disciples when they criticized the woman for "wasting" money that could be given to the poor. He said, "You always have the poor with you, and you can show kindness to them whenever you wish, but you will not always have me." Was he criticizing them for their concern for the poor?

We find that hard to imagine! Throughout his ministry, Jesus proclaimed God's concern for all people who live on the margins of society. In Matthew's parable of the Last Judgment, those who fed the hungry, gave drink to the thirsty, and clothed the naked were welcomed into God's eternal dominion (25:31–45). To a person who asked what to do to inherit eternal life, Jesus replied, "Go, sell what you own and give the money to the poor, and you will have treasure in heaven" (Mark 10:21). When John the Baptist sent word to Jesus from prison asking, "Are you the one who is to come?" Jesus answered him by offering him evidence of the coming of God's reign: "Go and tell John what you hear and see. The blind receive their sight, . . . the poor have good news brought to them" (Matt. 11:2–6). Jesus' concern for the poor was well known to all who followed him. He could not have been criticizing the disciples for caring about the poor!

Caring for the poor was not the issue. What Jesus condemned was the disciples' whole way of *seeing*. In particular, they saw relationship with God in terms of rules and requirements.

Jesus had often criticized the Jewish scribes and Pharisees for their legalistic interpretation of the law. First-century Judaism spelled out complex rules and codes that affected virtually every aspect of daily life. Jesus accused the religious authorities of making the fine points of the law more important than the purpose of the law, which was loving God and others. Jesus broke the laws of Judaism in several ways, including healing on the Sabbath and eating with sinners and outcasts. By sharing a meal at Bethany with Simon, a leper or former leper, Jesus was breaking one of the rules. Lepers, whether cured or not, were social outcasts, and contact with them made a person ritually impure. When the Pharisees had attacked Jesus for breaking the laws of Judaism, Jesus had called them hypocrites. He had said, "You tithe mint, dill, and cumin, and have neglected the weightier matters of the law: justice and mercy and faith. . . . You strain out a gnat but swallow a camel!" (Matt. 23:23–24).

Now Jesus' disciples were doing same thing Jesus had so often accused the scribes and Pharisees of doing. They turned Jesus' concern for the poor into a law, and they were busy focusing on the letter of that law.

The Blindness of Self-Righteousness

The trouble with seeing relationship with God in terms of requirements is that it tends to produce a very self-centered perspective. We obey the law in order to gain favor with God. "I will

help a neighbor in need in order to make myself right with God."
"I give to the poor in order to feel good about myself." A religion
of requirements tends to focus our attention on ourselves. Our
concern for our own self-righteousness can blind us to the real circumstances, sensitivities, and needs of another person.

We can hear self-righteousness in the disciples' comments
about the woman who anointed Jesus' head with expensive perfume. "'Why was this ointment wasted in this way? For this ointment could have been sold for more than three hundred denarii
and the money given to the poor.' And they scolded her" (Mark
14:4–5). Once we adopt an attitude of self-righteousness, it only
takes a tiny step to move to the condemnation of others. The disciples criticized the woman for doing what they had failed to do.
Their "righteous judgment" became a substitute for compassion.

Self-righteousness can be a way of dealing with our own sense
of guilt, a way to excuse our inaction in the face of the suffering
of others. How often have you heard comments like these:

- "I work hard for what I have. Let the poor do the same."
- "AIDS is God's punishment."
- "He made his bed; let him lie in it."
- "If she hadn't smoked all her life, she probably wouldn't have
  cancer."
- "If they had disciplined their son when he was younger, he
  wouldn't be on drugs now."
- "If you had picked up your toys when you were finished with
  them, you wouldn't have tripped over them and skinned your
  knee."
- "It's too bad their children are hungry, but that's what happens
  when babies are born out of wedlock."

Self-righteous judgment can be a substitute for compassion.
One time when the Pharisees criticized Jesus' disciples for breaking the purity laws, Jesus called them hypocrites and quoted
Isaiah: "This people honors me with their lips but their hearts are
far from me" (Mark 7:5–6). He might have said the same thing to
the critics of the woman at Bethany. They honored Jesus with

their lips. They held up one of his teachings—giving money to the poor—and condemned the woman for "breaking this law." But Jesus saw that their hearts were far from him.

Seeing with the Heart

This story is not about laws and requirements, whether they have to do with caring for the poor or with any other aspect of our lives. This story is about a larger issue. It is about seeing with our hearts. At Bethany two days before the Passover, as the chief priests and scribes were plotting ways to arrest Jesus and kill him, the one who needed compassion was Jesus himself. The woman who anointed his head with expensive perfume saw the reality of Jesus' circumstances and needs. She saw with her heart.

In all the Gospels, this is the only account we have of anyone who said goodbye to Jesus. The woman of Bethany said it with an act of incredible love. She might not have thought of her action as anointing Jesus' body for burial, even though that was Jesus' interpretation. But she clearly wanted to show her love to Jesus during his last days.

In the first chapter of this book, we saw the disciples do their best to deny Jesus' impending death, as if by denying that truth they could change it. Now at Bethany, the disciples didn't seem any closer to accepting the fact that Jesus must die. This woman alone had the courage to face the truth. With eyes of compassion, she saw the pain that lay ahead for Jesus. She felt as her own his loneliness as he headed down the road that ultimately he would have to walk alone. Her heart took it all in.

How natural it is to deny the reality of approaching death! When we learn that someone who is close to us has a terminal illness, our impulse is to close our eyes to the suffering, loneliness, and pain. We feel helpless. We don't know what to say, and so we may bounce in with false optimism. "Oh, you're going to get better!" we say with forced joviality. Or we may simply stay away.

A member of our congregation—call him Hank—once asked me to visit his mother in the hospital. "She has terminal cancer," he told me, "and she seems to need a kind of help that I'm not able to give her."

When I went to see Hank's mother, I found a woman who was mentally and emotionally healthy in spite of the deterioration of her body. She thought Hank was the one with a problem! "Hank is having a hard time accepting the fact that I am going to die," she said. "He won't let me talk about it."

After our visit, I sat down with Hank. "Were you able to help Mom?" he asked.

"I had a wonderful visit with her," I said, "and we had some very honest conversation. But the help she most needs must come from you. The essence of what your mother said to me is this: She loves you, and she has shared the most important parts of her life with you. Now, she wants to share her dying with you, too."

When we see with our heart, we gain the strength to look into the face of suffering instead of averting our eyes and pretending "it just isn't true." When we see with our heart, we stop trying to tell ourselves, "This doesn't concern me." We recognize that the pain of another person is our pain too. The woman who anointed Jesus' head with expensive perfume saw the situation as it really was. Seeing with her heart, she was able to discern what she could do. And *she did what she could.*

Even when we gain the courage to look into the face of suffering, we often fail to do anything about it. Part of the problem is discernment. We don't see what we can do. We know we can't fix all the problems we can identify. Hank couldn't cure his mother's illness. We can't feed all the hungry people in the world, or even all those in our community. We can't stamp out racism. We can't stop all war. We can't eliminate all the drugs from our streets or prevent all teenagers from becoming pregnant. We can't fix the problems of our children or our parents or our friends. We sometimes feel a sense of helplessness so overwhelming that it paralyzes us.

The woman at Bethany must have felt this helplessness. She knew she could not stop the forces that would lead to Jesus' death. But there was something she could do. The knowledge that she couldn't do everything did not blind her to the something that she could do.

Seeing with her heart, she was able to discern what would be helpful and what would not. She did not try to "solve" Jesus' "problem" or tell him what to do. She did not try to dissuade him from making the journey that he saw as his destiny, as we watched Peter do in the last chapter. She simply did what *she* could do.

Like the woman of Bethany, we know there are many things we cannot do. But we can do something. When we see with our hearts, we can discern the something that we can do. We can reach out to one or two people who need our help. We can join with churches and other agencies in their effort to help those in need. We can work toward changing social structures that foster racism and injustice. We can be present with a person in pain. We can listen to our children, our parents, our friends. We can offer an encouraging word, a friendly touch, an understanding smile or tear.

When we look with our hearts, we can assess our own unique gifts and ask, "What is the something that *I* can do?" We are able to distinguish between what we can and cannot do, what is helpful and what is not.

The woman of Bethany moved from discernment to action. She *did* what she could do. She gave an extravagant gift, a costly gift. But she didn't think of it in terms of cost. The point of the story is not that the gift was expensive. The point is that her gift came from her heart. When she saw the one thing that she could do, cost became irrelevant. Her gift was without price. What mattered to Jesus was not the cost of the gift; it was the love behind the gift. Her gift of love genuinely comforted and pleased Jesus. And he gave her his words of highest praise: "She has performed a good [or beautiful] service for me."

Living the Story

1. Pretend you are the woman in this story, and you are telling a very close friend about your experience. Be sure to tell your

friend how you *felt* at different parts of the story. Then tell the same story as if you were one of the disciples. Now tell it from Jesus' point of view.

2. In what ways do you wish to be like the woman in this story?
3. What part of you, like the disciples in this story, prevents you from being more like her?
4. What do you think Jesus might say to the voices of "the disciples" who are inside of you?
5. Do you agree that in this story the disciples substituted self-righteousness for compassion? What examples of substituting self-righteousness for compassion do you see in your own life? What examples do you see in the life of your congregation, your community, or the wider society? What is one thing you could do to show compassion in one of these situations?
6. What are some outward signs of persons who "see with their hearts"?
7. Meditate on the following poem.

Alabaster Jar

MYRA NAGEL

Priceless jar
broken
poured out
for him.
No thought of cost.
How extravagant!
How extravagant!

Priceless life
broken
poured out
for us.
No thought of cost.
How extravagant!
How extravagant!

This Week

Picture someone you know who is facing pain. Perhaps that person is sick or facing death. Perhaps he or she has lost a family member or close friend. Perhaps she or he has made a serious mistake, costing job or reputation. Visualize that person. Try to imagine yourself in that person's shoes. How might he or she feel? What would helpful? What would not be helpful? Compare your feelings about reaching out to this person with the feelings you described in no. 1, above. How are your feelings like the woman's? Like the disciples'? Like Jesus'? Decide on one thing you can do to help or comfort the person you visualized.

3

"You Will All Fall Away"

Coming to the Story

1. Close your eyes and try to picture the apostle Peter. Why do you think Jesus chose Peter as a disciple? Close your eyes again and try to picture Judas. Why do you think Jesus chose Judas as a disciple? (The Gospels do not give many details about Judas, so let your imagination run free.)
2. Read about Judas' betrayal and Peter's denial of Jesus in Mark 14:10–31, 66–72.
3. Where do you see yourself in this story?

Reflecting on the Story

In the first two stops along our journey to the cross, we saw Jesus trying to heal the blindness of his disciples. In the first chapter, Peter, James, and John finally recognized Jesus as the Christ, God's Messiah, but they expected him to rule the world in glory. They did not want to believe that the way of God's Messiah would be the way of suffering and death.

In the second chapter, we heard Jesus say again that he would die. He praised the woman of Bethany, who saw with her heart and anointed his body for its burial. Now the shadow of the cross lengthens. It looms before Jesus and his disciples.

After the scene at Bethany, the focus shifts to Judas Iscariot, and the theme shifts to human betrayal. Judas, one of the twelve disciples, went to the chief priests in order to betray Jesus to them. The chief priests were very pleased. They wanted to arrest Jesus in a place away from the crowds who had come to Jerusalem to celebrate the Jewish Passover, fearing that his arrest might cause a riot among the people (Mark 14:2). Judas agreed to provide them this opportunity. They promised to give Judas money, and the deal was struck.

"One of You Will Betray . . ."

The next scene addresses the subject of betrayal. Jesus wanted to celebrate the Passover meal with his disciples. As they began to eat, Jesus said, "Truly I tell you, one of you will betray me, one who is eating with me." The disciples were distressed and said to him, one after another, "Surely, not I?" (Mark 14:18–19).

But Judas had already struck his deadly bargain with the chief priests. Jesus had chosen Judas to be one of his closest followers. And yet he betrayed Jesus. Why? Christians have asked this question for twenty centuries. The Gospel stories don't give us a definitive answer. Still, we want to know, not because we care so much why Judas did it, but because Jesus' words haunt us. "One of you will betray me." Like the disciples we respond, "Surely, not I!"

To ask the question, "Why did Judas betray?" helps us to ask more important questions. What forces can and do cause close followers of Jesus to betray him? What could cause *us* to betray him? As we try to get inside the mind of Judas, we may be led to look honestly at blind spots within ourselves.

Scholars have suggested three primary motives for Judas' betrayal: (1) he did it for money; (2) he did it to ally himself with the power structure of his day; or (3) he did it to try to force Jesus into leading a revolution that would overthrow the Roman government by force. Let's look briefly at each of these possibilities.

Money?

Money is the most obvious motive for Judas' betrayal. Mark and Luke say the chief priests gave Judas money. Matthew specifies that they gave him thirty pieces of silver, a detail that reflects a prophecy from the book of Zechariah (11:12). John portrays Judas as a thief who stole from the disciples' common purse (13:29). Thus all four Gospels make some reference to money as the reason for Judas' betrayal.

Would *we* betray Jesus for money? Would our love of material things blind us to God's will for us?

Jim Wallis, in *A Call to Conversion*, offers this sobering idea: "That which commands our time, energy, and thoughts is what we really worship. The things we usually think about, worry over, and plan for are the things we value most."[1] What commands our time, energy, and thought? Our jobs? Our desire for a beautiful home, a new car, nice clothes? Our need to succeed and to raise successful children? In a sense, our checkbook is a statement of faith. Our daily calendar, where we record the ways we spend our time, can also be a statement of faith.

In the larger society, the laws we enact are a statement of faith. Would Jesus think that laws that preserve our environment for future generations are too expensive? What would he think about tax structures that offer a disproportionate advantage to the wealthy? What would he say about health care for the poor?

The majority of the people who are below the poverty line in our society are single mothers and their children. And the poorest of the poor are the single-parent families who come from ethnic minorities. If we benefit from the social structures that create this disparity of wealth, it is easy to turn a blind eye to the injustice. We may not even recognize the ways we participate in it.

Did Judas betray Jesus for money? We will never know. But asking that question urges us to answer these more important questions: What do we value most? What is our vision for our lives? What is our vision for our society?

Whether or not Judas betrayed Jesus for money, the important question is, "Would we?"

Conformity?

While money almost certainly was involved in Judas' betrayal, I find it difficult to believe that money was his only motive. For one thing, if Matthew was correct about thirty pieces of silver, the amount of money Judas received was not large. Under ten dollars or four pounds sterling, it was the purchase value of a slave. And if Judas had been motivated entirely by greed, why would he have joined a band of penniless followers of an itinerant preacher who proclaimed good news to the poor and who commanded his disciples not even to carry two shirts or an extra pair of sandals for their journey (Matt. 10:10)? It seems unlikely that money was Judas' only motivation.

Another possibility is that Judas wanted to ally himself with the people in power in his society, and that he betrayed Jesus in order to win their favor.

A person could not be a follower of Jesus and still conform to the expectations of the people who held the power in his society. Jesus infuriated the religious leaders by valuing compassion over strict adherence to their rituals and purity codes. He offended the wealthy by exhorting them to give up their riches and care for the poor. Jesus welcomed those whom society considered second-class citizens and even outcasts. He called disciples from the underclasses—fishers and common laborers. Some of his closest followers and friends were women, who were viewed by the society as mentally and physically inferior beings, the property of their fathers and husbands. He touched lepers; he ate with the ritually unclean; he kept company with the hated tax collectors. Jesus attacked the rich and powerful for hypocrisy, greed, and lack of compassion. No followers of Jesus could conform to the social pressures of their society. Perhaps Judas was trying to meet the expectations of the powerful and respected people of his day.

Would we betray Jesus to conform to social pressure?

Like Judas, we face social pressures. Some of the strongest influences are economic, as we have seen. And other social forces tempt us to betray our deepest values. There are the peer pressures on the young to smoke, to use alcohol, to do drugs, to succeed even if it involves cheating, to use sex as a badge of being "grown up," to join violent gangs. There are the social pressures on men and women of all ages to keep up with their neighbors, to be liked, to choose friends among the successful and popular, to look like they do and do what they do. Some pressures come from within the family. We see them in the middle-aged man still living out his parents' dreams for him, in the young adult still competing with his brother or her sister, in the wife whose values, desires, and politics are an unquestioning reflection of her husband's.

We do not know whether Judas' motive for betraying Jesus was the pressure to conform and to ally himself with the powerful. But we do know that the values of our society have a profound effect on the way we see ourselves. The pressures that were on Judas exist in our time, too.

Trust in Violence?

One of the most interesting suggestions biblical scholars have made about Judas' motive for betraying Judas is that he wanted to force Jesus into declaring that he was God's Messiah and leading a revolution that would overthrow the Roman government by force. Perhaps Judas was a member of the "zealot" party, a fanatical nationalist group whose goal was to drive out the Roman occupation forces through guerrilla tactics. One of the other disciples was Simon the Zealot.[2] Was Judas, like Simon, a zealot? For centuries the Jewish people had expected the coming of a Messiah, a leader who would overthrow Israel's oppressors and restore the nation to the glory it had known under King David. Was Judas disappointed because Jesus refused to lead a revolt against the Romans?[3] Did he betray Jesus in order to force his hand? Although there is no clear biblical evidence to prove this theory, many scholars think it is the most plausible motive.

The Jewish people chafed under the rule of the Roman Empire. Although Rome's official policy allowed Jews and other ethnic groups to live according to their own laws and customs, Rome kept order by military occupation and heavy taxation. For common people like the followers of Jesus, everyday worries included the threat of losing their land and livelihood because of high taxes. Rome granted citizenship to the aristocracies of conquered territories, but poorer people could not fulfill the requirements for citizenship. Perhaps Judas, a zealot like Simon, betrayed Jesus, believing he could force him to take the government into his own hands.

Do we betray Jesus by our reliance on the use of force?

Evil is as much a reality in our world today as it was in the time of Jesus. For our society and for each of us personally, the temptation to fight oppression and evil with force is very strong. We want to get back at those who hurt us, to get even, to "teach 'em a lesson." Think about the movies we watch and the books we read. The vast majority revolve around "getting the bad guys." Rarely do we see or read any other ways of resisting wrongdoing.

When I was a child, my father used to tell me bedtime stories about "bad boys who learned to be good." (In my four-year-old's perception of reality, the errant one was always a boy!) In these tales, something dreadful always happened to the bad boy, and as a result, he learned to be good. One night my father tried to change the plot. The boy's "victim" reached out to him in an act of compassion and forgiveness that caused the bad boy to change. I didn't like that ending! I wanted just retribution! I insisted that my father revise the conclusion of the story.

The urge to extract "an eye for an eye" is deeply imbedded in the human psyche. But in real life, retribution rarely helps "bad boys" learn to be good. What happens instead is that one angry word or deed provokes an equally angry response, and hatred and rage turn into a cycle. Vengeance becomes a way of thinking. Soon violence is a habit, a habit that is formed not only by the acts we perform but also by the violence that is done to us. Children who have been abused have a high probability of growing up to be abusers themselves. People who have been terrorized often retain such feelings of anger and righteous indignation that they adopt terrorizing patterns of vengeance themselves.

I don't want to minimize the complexity of the problems we face or the ills with which our society must deal. I don't want to underrate the pain of victims or to suggest that we should not resist evil. Jesus made it clear, after all, that we do have enemies and that we should resist them. But I do believe that the way we choose to respond to injustice is profoundly affected by the way we see our world. Perhaps human beings have already become so accustomed to wrongdoing that patterns of hatred and violence can't be unlearned. Perhaps brute force is the only way to cope with the evil in the world. Perhaps our only choice is to try to use violence more effectively and justly than anyone else. That is one worldview. Perhaps it is the way Judas saw the realities of human nature.

But Jesus had a different vision. Jesus chose another way. Was that the reason Judas struck a bargain with the chief priests?

We don't know why Judas betrayed Jesus. But as we try to imagine his motive, perhaps we will gain the courage to confront the Judas that lives within ourselves.

"You Will Deny Me . . ."

Judas was not the only one who would let Jesus down. After Jesus and his disciples shared the Passover meal, which we will look at more closely in the next chapter, they walked to the Mount of Olives. There Jesus said to them, "You will all become deserters," or as the Revised Standard Version translates it, "You will all fall away" (Mark 14:27).

Peter reacted immediately. He was a passionate man, the acknowledged leader of the disciples. He was enthusiastic, impetuous, and bold, at least on the surface. We can imagine him drawing himself to his full height and saying, "Even though all become deserters, I will not!"

And we can hear Jesus' quiet reply. "Before the cock crows, you will deny me three times."

Peter's response was filled with bravado. "I will never deny you. Even though I must die with you, I will not deny you" (Mark 14:29–31).

Throughout this story, as in the stories we read in the first two chapters, Jesus' clear vision stands in sharp contrast to the blindness of his disciples. Jesus saw his disciples perfectly. But they refused to see themselves. None of us want to see the parts of ourselves that betray, deny, or desert. How easy it is to close our eyes!

The disciples accompanied Jesus to the Garden of Gethsemane to pray. (We will look more closely at this part of the story in chapter 5.) While Jesus was still conversing with eleven of the disciples, Judas arrived, accompanied by a "crowd." With a kiss, he betrayed Jesus into the hands of the crowd, which was probably a motley band, hastily armed and sent by the religious authorities. They took Jesus to appear before the Jewish high priest. Peter followed at a distance, not wanting to be seen with Jesus. We may criticize Peter for following from such a distance, but he was the only one who followed at all. The others had all fallen away, just as Jesus said they would.

Peter got as far as the open courtyard at the household of the high priest. Others were there too, soldiers perhaps, as well as bystanders and servants. A servant said to Peter, "You were with Jesus, the man from Nazareth." Peter said quickly, "I don't know what you're talking about!"

Then the servant began to point at him and say to the bystanders, "This man is one of them." Now Peter was really frightened. Again he denied that he knew Jesus. Perhaps he made some conversation, trying to collect his thoughts. One of the bystanders recognized his accent and said, "Certainly you are one of them; you're a Galilean!" Now Peter's back was against the wall, and he said with a curse and an oath, "I do not know this man you are talking about" (14:66–71).

Cowardice or Helplessness?

I have always seen the account of Peter's denial as a story about a tragic loss of courage. But in recent days, I have been trying to "walk in Peter's shoes." I have asked myself, "If I had been there, what would I have done?" A strange thing happened to me as I tried to imagine myself in Peter's situation. I found myself defending Peter and the action he took. "What choice did he have?" I wondered. Suppose he'd made a different choice. Suppose when that servant woman came to him, he had stopped, taken a deep breath, and answered, "You're right, I was with Jesus." What then? Would his courage have made a difference? Could he have done anything to change what happened? What if he had been arrested and thrown into jail? Would he have been crucified with

Jesus? Might there have been four crosses instead of three? How would the story of the Christian church be different if Peter had not been there to lead it?

I like the serenity prayer attributed to Reinhold Niebuhr, which begins, "God grant me the serenity to accept the things I cannot change, courage to change the things I can, and wisdom to know the difference."[4] Did Peter's situation call for serenity to accept a situation he couldn't change? Or did it call for more courage? Was there something he might have changed?

We don't know the answer to any of these questions. But we can certainly identify with Peter's dilemma. As I have tried to walk in his shoes, I have come to believe that his denial of Jesus had its source in a feeling of helplessness. And I identify with that sense of helplessness.

During the years I lived and worked in the Washington, D.C., area, I went to a meeting once a month that took place at First United Church of Christ in the heart of the District of Columbia. I always hated making the trip. First Church was two blocks from the Metro station, and every time I walked those blocks, I was approached by a number of street people, asking for money. As I looked at them, I had a deep feeling of helplessness. Sometimes I found some change; other times I didn't. Whatever I did, I felt helpless. Their needs were so great. Anything I could do was so inadequate. And inside myself I wept, even as I denied.

We can identify with Peter and the helplessness he felt. We can understand his lack of courage. We can visualize Peter in the courtyard of the high priest. We can understand why he spoke those awful words: "I do not know the man you are talking about."

"Peter Remembered Jesus' Words"

Peter heard the cock crow. The sound pierced the night, and it must have pierced Peter's heart. He remembered the words of Jesus, "Before the cock crows twice, you will deny me three times." And Peter wept bitterly (14:72).

We can understand why Peter wept when he remembered the words of Jesus. We, too, remember the words of Jesus. We remember what Jesus said about conforming to materialism and the other values of our society:

"Blessed are you who are poor, for yours is the dominion of heaven" (Luke 6:20).

"No one can serve two masters . . . you cannot serve God and wealth" (Matt. 6:24).

"Where your treasure is, there will your heart be also" (Matt. 6:21).

"Truly I tell you, just as you did it to one of the least of these who are members of my family, you did it to me" (Matt. 25:40).

"[My followers] do not belong to the world, just as I do not belong to the world" (John 17:14).

We remember the words Jesus said about the ways we should treat others, including our enemies:

"You shall love God with all your heart, and with all your soul, and with all your mind. This is the greatest and first commandment. And a second is like it: You shall love your neighbor as yourself" (Matt. 22:37–40).

"Love your enemies and pray for those who persecute you. . . . For if you love those who love you, what reward do you have? Do not even the tax collectors do the same? . . . Be perfect therefore, as [God] is perfect" (Matt. 5:43–48).

We also remember Jesus' words about our feeling of helplessness:

"If you have faith the size of a mustard seed, you will say to this mountain, 'Move from here to there,' and it will move; and nothing will be impossible for you" (Matt. 17:21).

As we imagine Peter, standing in the open courtyard of the household of the high priest, denying his Christ three times, we, too, remember words of Jesus. And in our imagination we, like Peter, hear the cock crow.

When Peter remembered the words of Jesus, he broke down and

wept. Finally, he saw himself with clear eyes. Gone was the bluster that had caused him to rebuke Jesus for explaining that the way of the Messiah was the way of the cross. Gone was the bravado and the self-deceit that had caused him to say, "Even though I must die with you, I will not deny you." When Peter took off his blinders and looked at himself, he could do only one thing: he broke down and wept.

We grieve with Peter. We grieve for all the ways we have betrayed and denied and deserted. We grieve for hurts that we have inflicted and opportunities to do good that we have missed.

We know Peter's story does not end with his denial and the sound of the cock's crowing. Nor are betrayal, denial, and desertion the end of our story as disciples of Jesus. Although at times we may feel like Jesus' followers who asked in despair, "Then who can be saved?" we remember the words Jesus said to those followers: "For mortals it is impossible, but not for God; for God all things are possible" (Mark 10:23–27).

The focus of this chapter has been on human betrayal, denial, and desertion. But interwoven in Mark's story of human failure is the faithfulness of Jesus. We have been looking at human action; in the next chapters we will look at God's action. Let us not, however, move too quickly past this part of the story. Let us not skip lightly over the words, "Peter broke down and wept." Let us not close our eyes to the ways that both Judas and Peter live within us.

For our grief is the beginning of healing.

Living the Story

1. Recall your answers to "Coming to the Story," question 1, which asked why you think Jesus chose Judas and Peter as disciples and what he hoped for them. Why do you think Jesus chose you as his disciple? What were—and are—his hopes for you?
2. Remembering Jesus' hopes for you, imagine yourself talking to Jesus face-to-face about your life as his disciple. What might

you tell him that would make you weep? What might Jesus say about his love for you and your worth as a person? What might he say about forgiveness? What might he tell you to do—or to stop doing—now?

3. When you have done something you regret deeply, how is weeping the beginning of healing? What else do you need to do?

4. Consider again Jim Wallis's statement, "That which commands our time, energy, and thoughts is what we really worship." Reflect on the ways you spend your time, energy, and thoughts.

5. Judas wanted something else more than he wanted Jesus. What do you want more than you want Jesus?

6. Suppose the risen Christ had a conversation with Peter about his denial. Write a dialogue about what they might say. Then read the account of a conversation between Peter and the risen Christ in John 21:15–19. What does it have in common with the dialogue you wrote? How is it different? How might you change your dialogue after reading John's account?

7. Write a prayer of confession.

8. Meditate on the words of 1 John 1:8–9: "If we say we have no sin, we deceive ourselves, and the truth is not in us. If we confess our sins, [God] who is faithful and just will forgive us our sins and cleanse us from all unrighteousness."

This Week

Repeating a very short prayer sentence can create an inner stillness and thus help us listen to the voice of God. Every day this week, take five to fifteen minutes to meditate in the following way: Close your eyes and repeat over and over the prayer, "Jesus Christ, have mercy on me." End your meditation by repeating several times the assurance of God's forgiveness from 1 John in no. 8 above.

4

"Do This, Remembering Me"

Coming to the Story

1. Recall some of the times in your life when you have gathered at a table with people you love. Visualize the faces of those who were present. Remember the way you felt. How have these times of sharing food and companionship influenced your life?
2. Reread the story of the last meal Jesus shared with his disciples in Mark 14:10–31.
3. Where do you see yourself in this story?

Reflecting on the Story

In the last chapter we watched the disciples betray, deny, and fall away. One by one, they did the very thing they promised so boldly not to do. They abandoned Jesus in his hour of greatest need.

By the end of the story, Peter had come face to face with himself. He saw his own weakness with dreadful clarity. He had denied his Christ, and he wept bitterly. At that moment, Peter was healed of the blindness of self-deception, but another kind of blindness remained. Peter did not yet see fully the grace and power of God.

Human weakness is only one part of the account in Mark 14:10–50. Woven into the human story is God's story. Between the time when Jesus predicted the disciples' betrayal, denial, and desertion and the time when those predictions came true, Jesus drew his disciples into communion with him to celebrate a last meal together. As the shadow of the cross finally forced the disciples to look honestly at their own weakness and sin, Jesus also wanted to open their eyes to the power of God's grace.

How can God's story of grace change the human story of sin? We have looked at Mark 14:10–50 from the perspective of human betrayal. In this chapter and the next, we will examine it from the perspective of God's grace.

"Come to the Upper Room"

Immediately after Judas went to the chief priests to betray Jesus, Jesus instructed his disciples to prepare for the Passover meal. That evening, they came to an upper room to celebrate this traditional Jewish feast.

In the last chapter, we saw that the stories of Judas who betrayed, Peter who denied, and the other ten who deserted are our stories, too. This gathering in the upper room is also our story.

Imagine that you are a first-century Jewish person. Picture yourself in the upper room. See yourself and the other disciples partially reclining around a low table in the traditional manner for a meal of celebration. Imagine the faces of those who are gathered. There is Peter. That very night, Peter will fall away and deny Jesus. There is Andrew, Peter's brother. He, too, will fall away and disappear. See the faces of James and John, the sons of Zebedee. They are the ones who argued about who was the greatest and who asked Jesus to seat them in the place of honor at his right and left hand in his glory. They, too, will fall away. Imagine the expression on the faces of Philip, Bartholomew, Matthew the former tax collector, and Thomas, the one who doubted. They will all desert Jesus. James, the son of Alphaeus, is there, too, along with Thaddaeus and Simon the Zealot. They, too, will disappear into the night. And finally there is Judas Iscariot, the betrayer.[1]

Jesus speaks. "One of you will betray me," he says. "Peter, you will deny me three times. You will all become deserters." One after another, the disciples protest, "Surely not I?" Jesus looks at you. What do you say?

Jesus breaks bread and shares it with you and the other disciples. As you imagine this scene and picture yourself in it, you may think of the act of eating together as an ordinary thing, but it wasn't. In the time of Jesus, sharing a meal was not the casual act of sociability it is for us today. It had a significance that is hard for us to understand. To eat with someone was to accept that person. To gather at the same table was a sign not only of communion among people but also of communion in the sight of God. The Pharisees constantly criticized Jesus for eating with "tax collectors and sinners." No good Jew would eat with someone who was impure. By eating with sinners and outcasts, Jesus implicitly included them in a relationship of communion with God.

On the night he was betrayed, the sinners with whom Jesus broke bread were his own disciples. Jesus knew that they would all fall away before the night was over. Yet he drew them around his table. He drew them into a relationship of close community. Picture yourself there reclining at the table with them. Try to see Jesus' face. You see sadness in it, but also tenderness.

"Remember!"

As Jesus begins the Passover ritual, his words are so familiar to you that you can almost say them by heart. As a good Jew, you have celebrated this central feast of the Jewish faith year after year. The words of the ritual recall for you the story that is told in the book of Exodus (chap. 1–14). The story took place some thirteen centuries before the birth of Jesus. At that time, your Hebrew ancestors were slaves under the oppressive reign of the pharaoh of Egypt. God called Moses to lead them out of bondage. To persuade the pharaoh to release the Hebrew captives, God brought a series of plagues upon Egypt. In the last of these, Moses instructed all the Hebrew families to kill a sacrificial lamb and to put its blood on the doorway of their home. That night, God slew the firstborn of every Egyptian family, but God passed over the Hebrew families. When the pharaoh saw what God had done, he let the slaves go. Before they could get out of Egypt, however, he changed his mind. Just as the pharaoh's pursuing armies were nearly upon the fleeing Hebrews, God caused the waters of the Red Sea to separate. Your Hebrew ancestors passed over on dry land, while the pursuing Egyptian chariots were washed away in the returning waters.

Now as you listen to Jesus retell the story, the Exodus event comes to life in your imagination. In the Hebrew way of thinking, to *remember* did not simply mean to bring something back into one's mind. The Jewish rituals of remembering brought God's past action into the present. Remembering made a person a participant in the historic event. Each time the Jewish community celebrated Passover, they became the Hebrew slaves living under the oppressive reign of the pharaoh. They became the parents whose firstborn child was spared from death. They joined the band of refugees who crossed safely over the Red Sea and were nurtured by God's manna in the wilderness.

As you imagine yourself gathering with the disciples around a table with Jesus, try to remember the Passover as the disciples would have remembered it. Remember it as your own personal history. *You* were the Hebrew slave in Egypt. *You* sang a song of joy and thanksgiving from the safe side of the Red Sea. As you remember how God brought you out of slavery in Egypt, you sense God's freeing power alive in you now.

Hear Jesus' words. He gives thanks. With full knowledge of what lies ahead of him in the next few days, Jesus still gives thanks for God's graciousness and God's power to break the bondage in which human beings are enslaved. Jesus blesses the bread and the cup.

Then Jesus breaks the bread and says, "Take, eat. This is my body." Suddenly you see surprise on the disciples' faces. They look at Jesus, then at the bread, then back to Jesus, their eyes filled with questions. Is he saying that *he* is the lamb who is being sacrificed in this feast of thanksgiving for the power of God to break human bondage? Jesus continues, and you share the disciples' deepening amazement. He says, "This cup is my blood of the covenant which is poured out for many." Is Jesus actually saying his blood is poured out for you?[2]

The disciples do not understand Jesus' words. A few moments ago, they did not believe him when he said they would all fall away. Now they do not understand how his body and blood are to be poured out for them. They cannot understand; they are not yet able to look at this event from the perspective of Easter.

As we imagine ourselves in the upper room with Jesus and the disciples, we may share some of their bewilderment and identify with their lack of understanding. But unlike the disciples, we look back on this event from the perspective of Easter faith. In the light of Easter, we begin to perceive its significance with new eyes.

Jesus responded to the sin of his disciples by drawing them into closer communion with himself and with God. He imposed no conditions for this intimate relationship with God. Though he knew they would betray and desert him, he did not reject them. Instead, he drew them closer. He responded to their weakness by remembering God's power to break human bondage and by drawing them into that power in a radical new way. As we look from this side of Easter, we see the last meal Jesus shared with his disciples as a story of profound grace.

"Accept the Gift of Grace"

The Hebrew and Greek words for *grace* may also be translated *favor*. Noah found grace or favor in the eyes of God (Genesis 6:8). The people found grace or God's favor in the wilderness (Jeremiah 31:2). Jesus increased in favor or grace with God (Luke 2:52). Christians sometimes use *grace* interchangeably with *forgiveness*, but grace is a more inclusive term suggesting a right or favorable relationship with God. The apostle Paul wrote, "Since all have sinned and fall short of the glory of God, they are now justified by [God's] grace as a gift, through the redemption that is in Christ Jesus" (Rom. 3:23–24).

God's grace was not a new concept for the Jewish people. The law itself was God's gift to the newly freed Hebrew slaves to show them how to respond appropriately to God's gracious blessings.[3] Grace was not new, nor was the promise of God's forgiveness. But the Pharisaic Judaism of Jesus' day had come to see relationship with God in terms of stringent requirements rather than in terms of grace. Forgiveness was possible, but repentance and restitution were prior conditions.[4] As we saw in the story of the anointing at Bethany, the problem with a system that sees relationship with God in terms of requirements is that it tends to focus human beings' attention on themselves. "I will take a cake to my sick neighbor in order to gain God's favor." "I will apologize to my sister because God demands it of me."

Jesus upended Pharisaic Judaism's insistence on a relationship with God that was filled with conditions and requirements. Jesus responded to sinners by eating with them. He responded to his disciples' sin by drawing them into the intimate communion of the Passover meal even as he told them they would betray and deny and desert him. God's grace is unconditional. Relationship with God is simply a gift.

The disciples who celebrated the Passover meal with Jesus heard his words, but they did not understand what he said. They were too busy protesting that they would never betray or deny or fall away. They were blind, both to their own weakness and to the power of God's grace. Jesus' way of thinking was too radical for them.

Jesus' way of thinking seems radical to us, too. If God's grace is unconditional, does that mean we can follow our own selfish interests, secure in the knowledge that through Jesus Christ we are reconciled and made one with God? What about judgment and punishment? What about our need for repentance? What about the very real concerns of victims in our society and their right to restitution? What does unconditional grace say about sin, punishment, culpability, responsibility, and repentance?

These are important questions, and the answers are not simple. But Jesus' action provides us a framework for reflecting on them that is quite different from a perspective that sees relationship with God in terms of requirements. As Jesus shared the Passover meal with his disciples, he said to them, in effect,

"Come, join me in the celebration of God's power to break all human bondage. God is gracious. I am the sacrificial lamb of the Passover. My blood joins you with me in this sacrifice of thanksgiving. Take my body and my blood to you; they will join you with me in community with God and with one another." A relationship of grace does not focus on requirements; it brings about the transformation of our lives through an ever-deepening friendship with God.

A relationship of grace does not mean we will not sin. It does mean God will not turn away from us even in our sin. Grace does not free us from punishment, for sin brings its own punishment both for the sinner and for those who are sinned against. It does mean God will not abandon us even as we suffer punishment.

A relationship of grace does not remove the need for repentance or free us from doing everything we can to right the wrongs we have committed. But it does recognize that forgiveness cannot be earned, whether through repentance or through any other means.[5] And it changes our purpose for making amends. When we operate out of close communion with Christ, we begin to look at things from God's viewpoint. We see more clearly the pain we have caused others, and we feel that pain as our own. Our repentance is genuine, and our heartfelt desire is for the well-being of the person we have wronged. Seeing from Christ's perspective deepens our compassion and allows us insight into the real feelings and needs of another person, not because we are trying to find favor with God, but because we genuinely care.

Whenever we come to the communion table remembering the last meal Jesus shared with his disciples, we lay claim to the thinking of our ancestors of the Hebrew faith. To remember is to be there. To remember is to join the disciples around the table with Jesus as our host, to eat the bread he breaks for us, to drink the cup he pours out for us, and to hear the words he wants us to understand. "Take and eat. I know you have betrayed, denied, and deserted, and you will do it again. I know you have failed to love God fully and to love your neighbor as yourself. And you will fail again. But come to me. Join with me. Take to yourself my body and my blood. In communion with me, you will find power to break the bondage of your self-centeredness and your weakness."

Even as we accept the gift of God's grace and begin to feel the strength to break our own patterns of destructive thinking and acting, we may wonder, "How do I deal with those who do wrong to me?" What about the power of evil in the world? What does the sharing of bread mean to the woman who lives with a husband who is physically or emotionally abusive? What does the sharing of a cup say to a teenage boy who is trapped in the inner-city neighborhood he sees as a dead end? What do the words of Jesus say to the employee whose sex, race, or sexual orientation is considered more important than ability and experience? What does the sacrament of Holy Communion say to members of a community whose water supply is threatened by the pollution created by a powerful industry?

"Behold God's Power"

Again, answers are not simple. But if we truly *remember*, in the Hebrew sense of being there, we remember that evil was as much a reality for the disciples of Jesus as it is for us today. They were in bondage to the Romans. They were oppressed by a social structure that excluded them from material benefits and social status. The forces of evil in their society conspired to crucify Jesus. Yet on the night he was betrayed, Jesus remembered the Passover with his disciples. They told the familiar story, not in the past tense, but in the present. Perhaps they told it in words similar to these from Deuteronomy.

> When the Egyptians treated us harshly and afflicted us, by imposing hard labor on us, we cried to . . . the God of our ancestors; [God] heard our voice and saw our affliction, our toil, and our oppression. [God] brought us out of Egypt with a mighty hand and an outstretched arm, with a terrifying display of power, and with signs and wonders; and [God] brought us into this place and gave us this land, a land flowing with milk and honey. (26:5–9)

Whenever we come to the table of Holy Communion, we remember that God does not want us to remain in situations that are oppressive and destructive. We remember that God calls us to resist the power of evil. We remember God's power to free us from bondage, whether it is the bondage of our own sin, the bondage of a destructive relationship, the bondage of racism or sexism, or the bondage of economic domination. In the next three chapters we will learn more about God's power, and we will see how the disciples eventually connected with it and made it their own.

Whenever we come to the table of Holy Communion, we remember that we are invited into community with Christ, with God, and with one another. We remember that Christ's words are an invitation, not a command. God will not retract the invitation, even if we reject it. We can separate ourselves from God, but God will not separate from us. We remember that Christ invites us into communion without requirements. We remember also that Christ calls the church to be a community of unconditional love and to include those individuals whom society rejects. We remember the power of the risen Christ, and we feel that power alive and at work within and among us.

A clergy friend once told me of an incident that took place while he was celebrating communion in his congregation. He had issued the traditional invitation and was about to ask the deacons to come forward to distribute the bread and cup when a member of the congregation stood up. The pastor didn't know how to deal with this unprecedented interruption of the communion ritual. Before he could collect his thoughts, the man began to speak, his voice breaking with emotion: "I am an alcoholic. Today I am going into a treatment center and I ask for your prayers, and your forgiveness." The pastor didn't say a word. But God did. For that congregation rose, to a person. They made their way to the man, surrounded him, and held him.

Such is the power of the community of Christ. Such is the power Christ invites us to receive. Such is the power God calls us to embody in the world. It is the power to change the future.

Living the Story

1. "Reflecting on the Story" invited you to imagine yourself in the upper room celebrating the Passover meal with Jesus and his disciples. Reread that portion of "Reflecting." Then close your eyes and bring the scene into your mind. Try to remember in the Hebrew sense of being there. What feelings or insights come from this remembering?

2. The Jewish Passover and the Christian sacrament of Holy Communion celebrate God's power to free us from bondage. What force within you seems to hold you in bondage? What keeps you from being the person you think God created you to be? Imagine yourself telling a trusted friend about this inner force. Then imagine yourself holding the same conversation with Jesus, remembering that Jesus knows you and loves you. Consider writing this dialogue or speaking it into a tape recorder.

3. How do you feel in bondage to a force or person outside yourself? As above, imagine yourself in conversation with Jesus about this bondage. What does Jesus say about his desires for you? How can your faith give you power to break free? What other help do you need? Where might you find this help?

4. How do you see God's power at work in the world to break down structures of bondage, oppression, and injustice? How can you connect with this power?

5. How do you understand the relationship between sin, repentance, and grace? How does accepting God's friendship as a gift seem different from viewing relationship with God in terms of requirements? How do you see this difference in specific situations in your life?

6. What is preventing you from accepting God's gracious gift of friendship?

7. How well is your church responding to God's call to be a community of grace? How might your church better embody the love of Jesus, who ate with sinners and outcasts and invited all people into communion with him?

8. Meditate on the words of John 6:35: "Jesus said to them, 'I am the bread of life. Whoever comes to me will never be hungry, and whoever believes in me will never be thirsty.'"

This Week

For at least one meal, set an extra place as a reminder that Christ is present at your table.

5

"Not What I Want, but What You Want"

Coming to the Story

1. Take a few minutes to reflect on your own prayer life. How would you describe it? How is prayer a sustaining force for you? What prevents you from having a fuller prayer life?
2. Reread Mark 14:32–42.
3. Where do you see yourself in this story?

Reflecting on the Story

Friendship with Christ is God's strategy for transforming the world and each individual life. That is Jesus' strategy for healing the blindness of his disciples and opening their eyes. In the last chapter, we watched Jesus draw his disciples into communion with him even as he told them they would betray, deny, and desert him. And we saw that God also invites us into this life-transforming friendship.

What might a life lived in close relationship with Christ be like? As if to answer that question, Jesus led his disciples to the Garden of Gethsemane to pray. A life lived in communion with Christ is a life of prayer.

In the Garden of Gethsemane, we see again the disciples' failure to understand and do all that Jesus asked of them. While Jesus went off by himself to pray, he asked Peter, James, and John to "keep awake"—in other words, to stay spiritually alert; stay tuned in to God. Jesus had used the same word when he commanded his disciples to keep alert and watch for the coming dominion of God (Mark 13:32–37). Jesus wanted his disciples to hold him in their consciousness and in so doing to link their spirits with God's. He might have said, "Pray for me, and pray for God's will in this situation." That is what he was asking them to do.

But in the Garden of Gethsemane, the disciples did not keep alert. They did not hold Jesus in their consciousness. They did not seek to know and follow the will of God. They did not pray, for themselves or for their Christ. Their strength had run out. Three times Jesus returned and found them sleeping.

Jesus' energy level must also have been at a low ebb, but he did not fall asleep! Instead, he opened himself to the strength and power of God. In his example, we find a model for our own lives.

Be Open

Jesus believed in the power of prayer. Do we truly believe in that power?

We are creatures of the modern age, an age of science, technology, and reason. Since the rise of rationalism and the scientific spirit in the seventeenth and eighteenth centuries, our culture has tended to place a high value on scientific analysis. If science can't explain something, it doesn't seem real to us. The act of prayer takes for granted a different concept of reality. It assumes the existence of mystery and power that we can't prove through science or analyze through reason. Prayer is not necessarily anti-science or anti-reason. But when we pray—when we really pray— we acknowledge the possibility of a dimension of reality that is beyond our ability to explain. And if we are to make prayer a way of life, we must open our whole being to that unexplained—and unexplainable—dimension.

Jesus had no uncertainty about the reality of God's presence. He had no question about the power of God. God was part of his everyday experience. Marcus Borg, in his insightful book *Meeting Jesus Again for the First Time*, states, "The most crucial fact about Jesus was that he was a 'spirit person,' a 'mediator of the sacred,' one of those persons in human history to whom the Spirit was an experiential reality."[1] He knew God so personally and intimately that he addressed God as "Abba," meaning "Daddy" or "Papa."

In preparation for every key decision of his life, Jesus spent time alone with God. Before he began his ministry, he went to the wilderness for an ordeal of spiritual temptation, out of which came a clearer formation of his spiritual vision. Luke tells us that before Jesus chose the disciples, he prayed on a mountain for an entire night (6:12–16). In preparation for the journey to Jerusalem, Jesus went to a mountain to pray, and he was transfigured in the presence of Peter, James, and John (Mark 9:2–8). Now, as Jesus prepared to face the greatest crisis of his life, we are not surprised to find him in the Garden of Gethsemane, opening his spirit to God in prayer.

If we open ourselves to God's spirit, if we don't close off our minds at the boundary of our ability to measure and explain, we can know a divine companion who will be with us in any and all situations. We can know the God that Jesus knew. Only our blindness keeps us from experiencing the energy, the power, and the mystery that can be ours through prayer.

Be Silent

In the Garden of Gethsemane, Mark tells us, Jesus spent hours alone with God, yet the words he prayed were breathtakingly simple: "Abba, Father, for you all things are possible; remove this cup from me; yet not what I want, but what you want" (Mark 14:36). Only twenty-two words in all that time!

I reached a breakthrough in my own spiritual life when I came to the realization that prayer for me consisted largely of talking to God. My role as a minister leading public worship exacerbated this tendency. One day I picked up *The Way of the Heart*, by Henri Nouwen, author of numerous books on spirituality and teacher of pastoral theology at Yale Divinity School. I recognized myself in his words.

> If the public prayers of ministers . . . are any indication of their prayer life, God is certainly busy attending seminars. How can we possibly expect anyone to find real nurture, comfort, and consolation from a prayer life that taxes the mind beyond its limits and adds one more exhausting activity to the many already scheduled ones? During the last decade, many have discovered the limits of the intellect. . . . They wonder how they might really experience God. . . . Suddenly we find ourselves surrounded by people saying, "Teach us to pray."[2]

Jesus did not try to reason his way to God, and his prayers were not filled with words. Mark summed up Jesus' prayer in the Garden of Gethsemane in one sentence: "Abba, Father, for you all things are possible; remove this cup from me; yet not what I want, but what you want." Earlier, when Jesus told the parable of the Pharisee and the tax collector, Jesus commended the tax collector's one-sentence prayer: "God be merciful to me, a sinner" (Luke 18:9–14). And when Jesus' disciples said to him, "Teach us to pray," Jesus responded with a prayer that was only five lines long, according to Luke's version, which is probably the most authentic:

> Father, hallowed be your name.
> Your kingdom come.
> Give us each day our daily bread.
> And forgive us our sins, for we ourselves forgive everyone
>   indebted to us.
> And do not bring us to the time of trial. (11:2–4)

I do not believe that Jesus intended for us to memorize these words and speak them by rote. I think he meant to suggest a general framework for our quiet attitudes of prayer:

• Focus attention on God.
• Turn yourself over to God's will.

- Ask for things you truly need.
- Ask God's forgiveness and seek to live in an attitude of forgiveness.
- Ask God to keep you from anything contrary to God's will.

The Prayer of Jesus was not a stream of words; it was a description of attitudes in which we are to sit in silence before God. When I began to try to empty my mind and sit in stillness before God, I immediately ran into a problem. Words would not leave me alone. They intruded themselves into my silence, taking my mind off in one direction and then another. Again, I found Nouwen's advice helpful. He suggests repeating a very simple sentence such as, "O God, come to my assistance," or "Jesus have mercy on me," or a single word such as "Jesus." "Such a simple, easily repeated prayer can slowly empty out our crowded interior life," he says, "and create the quiet space where we can dwell with God."[3] This kind of prayer moves from mental exercise to experience, from the mind to the heart.

Be Heart to Heart

Jesus and his disciples came to the Garden of Gethsemane with heavy hearts. And when hearts are aching, prayer is often difficult.

When I do counseling with persons who are struggling with pain, anger, or grief, I often ask, "How are you praying about your pain? How are you praying about your anger?" More often than not, they respond, "I haven't been able to pray at all." Their feelings are all negative, and they don't think God wants to hear those negative feelings. But no relationship can be intimate if it cannot be honest. Our attempt to hide "unacceptable" feelings prevents us from acknowledging before God what is truly in our hearts.

In the Garden of Gethsemane, the feelings of Jesus and his followers must have seemed like a catalog of the emotions human beings try to hide from God: terror, vulnerability, cowardice, hopelessness, despair, anger at their own people, rage at the authorities, even anger with God. Mark tells us that Jesus began to be deeply "distressed." Scholars have translated this word as "troubled," "agitated," "appalled," "feeling dread," and "terrified." Jesus faced agony that was greater than any he had ever known, not only because physical suffering lay ahead, but also because his own Jewish community had rejected him. Jesus told his disciples, "I am deeply grieved, even to death," meaning, "I am so sad I feel like I am going to die" (14:34).

The disciples dealt with their negative feelings by falling asleep! Luke's version of the story contains a fascinating psychological insight. Jesus found the disciples "sleeping *because of grief*" (22:45, emphasis added). Sleep was a way of escaping from the pain that was too heavy to bear.

In contrast, Jesus dealt with his negative emotions by turning them over to God. He threw himself on the ground. We don't know exactly what he said, but throwing oneself on the ground is clearly a gesture of abandon. It is not the posture of someone who was trying to hide his true feelings. Jesus turned over to God everything that was in his heart, his anguish, his desolation, and his desperation. He trusted that his heart would find acceptance in God's heart. "Prayer of the heart," says Nouwen, "challenges us to hide absolutely nothing from God and to surrender ourselves unconditionally to [God's] mercy."[4]

If we have trouble believing that God can accept us at our worst, we can turn to the book of Psalms. The Psalms are a collection of the prayers of the people of Israel, both individual and corporate, collected over several centuries. They are sincere, real, and sometimes raw. Look at the wail of pain in Psalm 77:

> I cry aloud to God that God may hear me. . . .
> "Will God spurn forever, and never again be favorable?
> Has God's steadfast love ceased forever?
> Are God's promises at an end for all time?
> Has God forgotten to be gracious?" (1, 7–8)

Psalm 13 doesn't try to hide the psalmist's anger at God:

> How long, O God? Will you forget me forever?
> How long will you hide your face from me?

How long must I bear pain in my soul,
and have sorrow in my heart all day long? (1–2)

And Psalm 22, the words Jesus spoke from the cross, is a cry of despair: "My God, my God, why have you forsaken me?"

The Psalms express many feelings that don't seem "worthy" to us. But they are honest. The people of Israel trusted their heart to the care of God's heart.

In the Garden of Gethsemane, Jesus threw himself on the ground and poured out his agony. Addressing God in the most intimate of terms, he prayed with desperate honesty for what he wanted. "Abba, for you all things are possible; remove this cup from me." The "cup" symbolized a person's fate.[5] Jesus' "cup" was death on the cross.

Who of us has not prayed passionately in moments of fright and anguish for God to "remove this cup"? I remember a time in the wee hours of the night when I asked God to spare the life of my father who was in the hospital with congestive heart failure. He had been my soulmate for nearly fifty years, and I could not imagine facing life without him.

When we pray out our anguish honestly before God, transformation takes place. Somehow, at some time during the hours when Jesus poured out his heart in anguish in the Garden of Gethsemane, his spirit breathed to God the words, "Yet not what I want, but what you want." We sense in these words a new feeling of acceptance, peace, and strength.

On the night when I begged God to spare the life of my father, I do not remember exactly when I began to sense a transformation in the state of my emotions. I prayed. I wept. I spent time with God in wordless anguish. Then at some point during that night, a different feeling came over me. It was as if a voice said, "You still have some precious time. Use it!"

Suddenly my thoughts and emotions began moving in a new direction. My father had directed a college theater in his professional life, and youthful actors and actresses still inhabited the stage of his memory. I remembered that my bookshelf held a copy of a one-act comedy by A. A. Milne that he had enjoyed directing.

The next day, my daughter and I sat at his bedside and read this play to him. My father's eyes lit up. At times he laughed. With strengthening voice, he joined us in several parts of the dialogue.

The days that followed were some of the most painful of my life but also some of the most cherished. My father and I shared stories, laughter, tears, words of love, and simple quiet companionship. When he died peacefully in his sleep a few weeks later, I received the news with great grief but also with a sense of triumph and a surprising feeling of peace. I have always been deeply grateful for that voice in the night that transformed the state of my inner being and showed me how to take the gift of those days to my heart.

When we pray out our anguish to God, transformation does take place. We see this transformation in the Psalms. The wail of pain in Psalm 77, which began, "Will God spurn forever?" ends with these words:

> "Your way, O God, is holy. . . .
> With your strong arm you redeemed your people. . . .
> You led your people like a flock." (vv. 13, 20)

Psalm 13, which began angrily, "How long, O God? Will you forget me forever?" ends in these words:

> "But I trusted in your steadfast love;
> my heart shall rejoice in your salvation.
> I will sing to God,
> because God has dealt bountifully with me." (vv. 5–6)

One of the best-known examples of the transformation from despair to hope is Psalm 22, which began with the words Jesus spoke from the cross, "My God, my God, why have you forsaken me?" The psalm ends in triumph:

> From you comes my praise in the great congregation. . . .
> The poor shall eat and be satisfied;
> those who seek God shall praise God. . . .

Future generations will be told about God
And proclaim God's deliverance to a people yet unborn.
  (vv. 25–26, 30–31)

In the Garden of Gethsemane, Jesus prayed out his anguish to God. Terror, agitation, distress, and dread became acceptance, peace, and strength. "Remove this cup from me" became, "Not what I want, but what you want." The story of the Garden of Gethsemane opens our eyes to the transformation that can take place in our lives when we let prayer flow honestly from our heart to God's heart.

Heart-to-heart prayer transforms our inner being and ultimately moves us to action. "'Enough,' Jesus said to the disciples. 'The hour has come. . . . Get up, let us be going.' He looked up and said, 'See, my betrayer is at hand'" (14:41–42).

In the next chapter, we will see Jesus live out his prayer, "Not what I want, but what you want." His relationship with God was so intimate that his life was inseparable from his consciousness of God's presence. His prayer became action. And his action became a prayer as Jesus walked into Good Friday, heart to heart with God.

Living the Story

1. Recall a time when prayer has been a very powerful experience for you. What made this experience so powerful?
2. Think back to your answer to "Coming to the Story," no. 1: "What prevents you from having a fuller prayer life?" What insights have you gained about your own prayer life by reading this chapter and the biblical account of the Garden of Gethsemane?
3. What decision, problem, or crisis are you facing right now? How are you praying about that decision or crisis? How might your prayer be more "heart to heart"?
4. Do any of the following words that described the feelings of Jesus and his disciples in the Garden of Gethsemane resonate

in your life right now: *fear, vulnerability, cowardice, hope-*
lessness, despair, anger at others, anger at God? If any of these
words resonate in your life, read Psalm 13:1–4. Using words
from the psalm or words of your own, decide on a short phrase
or question that voices some of your feelings. Sit quietly with
God, repeating that phrase. Then read the end of the psalm,
verses 5 and 6. Again choosing words from the psalm or words
of your own, frame a brief petition that asks God for your
heartfelt desire. Some examples are, "Let me feel your stead-
fast love"; "rejoice my heart"; "sing in my heart"; "save me."
Repeat your petition silently to God for several minutes.

5. Pray as described in no. 4 above, repeating the sentence Jesus
   prayed in the Garden of Gethsemane: "Not what I want, but
   what you want."

6. Meditate on the Prayer of Jesus. Find a time and space away
   from distractions. Read very slowly the Prayer of Jesus in Luke
   11:2–3. Choose one phrase or word that seems important to
   you at this moment. If you wish, restate it in your own words.
   Close your eyes and repeat this word or phrase very slowly to
   God. Do this for at least five minutes.

This Week

Pray daily in the manner described in nos. 4, 5, and 6 above. Each
day, choose a word or phrase from scripture that speaks to your
current struggles and emotions, restating it in your own words if
you wish. In a place and time free from distraction, repeat your
word or phrase in silence before God. The first day, pray in this
way for at least five minutes. Gradually extend the time each day
until you reach twenty or thirty minutes by the week's end.

6

"Crucify Him!"

Coming to the Story

1. What is your favorite Lenten hymn? "Go to Dark Gethsemane"? "When I Survey the Wondrous Cross"? "Ah, Holy
Jesus"? "O Sacred Head Now Wounded"? "Were You There?"
Sing or hum your favorite hymn, or say in your mind as many
of its words as you can. Play a tape recording of this hymn if
you have one, and let the words and music seep into your
spirit. If you have a hymnal, read the hymn slowly and
thoughtfully. What scene, word, or phrase touches your emotions? Spend several minutes repeating this word or phrase
slowly, aloud or silently, or imagine yourself in the scene that
moved you.
2. Read Mark 14:53–65, 15:1–47.
3. Where do you see yourself in this story?

Reflecting on the Story

One of my favorite Lenten hymns is the spiritual "Were You
There?"

Were you there when they crucified my Lord?
Were you there when they crucified my Lord?
Oh! Sometimes it causes me to tremble, tremble.
Were you there when they crucified my Lord?[1]

As our journey nears the foot of the cross, we could approach the story of the Crucifixion from many vantage points. We could see it as a fulfillment of Hebrew prophecy. We could view it through the eyes of the apostle Paul and other leaders of the early church. We could study the interpretations of Christian theologians through the centuries, including St. Augustine in the fourth century, Anselm and Thomas Aquinas in the twelfth century, and Martin Luther, Ulrich Zwingli, and John Calvin in the sixteenth century. All of these perspectives are significant for our faith. But in the space of these few pages, I suggest that we take a less complicated approach and simply try to enter the story as participants. Taking a cue from the hymn "Were You There?" let's try to experience the story through the eyes of some who were there.

As the story begins, notice who was *not* there. The disciples were conspicuously absent. Throughout the journey to the cross, Mark has portrayed the blindness of the disciples, and he has shown how Jesus tried to heal their blindness by leading them in the way of the cross. With Judas' betrayal and the scattering of the other eleven, Mark's portrait of the disciples' blindness is almost complete. For the final touch, Peter appears one last time and denies that he ever knew the man he had so recently called "the Christ." To the question, "Were you there when they crucified my Lord?" the disciples have answered, "No."

Deserted by his closest friends, Jesus faced his enemies alone. And Mark continues to paint the contrast between blindness and true vision.

The Chief Priests

The religious authorities—priests, elders, and scribes—had awaited their opportunity to trap Jesus. They wanted to get rid of him "legally," without stirring up a revolt in the crowds that were gathered in Jerusalem for the celebration of Passover. Judas handed them their opportunity. After Judas identified him with a kiss, the chief priests had Jesus arrested and taken to the home of the high priest for questioning.

As the head of the priesthood, the high priest presided over the Sanhedrin, the council of Jewish leaders that acted as a judicial court to interpret Jewish life, custom, and law. The examination of Jesus was probably not a regular trial involving the full membership of the Sanhedrin, but rather a private interrogation at the home of the high priest.[2]

The chief priests, elders, and scribes who assembled represented the religious and social hierarchy of Judaism. They took their religion seriously, following every letter of the law. Yet Jesus criticized them sharply throughout his ministry. He accused them of false pride, self-centeredness, and hardness of heart. He said they substituted righteousness for compassion; they kept the law to feel good about themselves and forgot the purpose of the law, which Jesus summed up in the commandments of loving God and others. Jesus called them hypocrites because they made a show of their prayers and fasting, going through the motions of worship while their hearts were far from God. No wonder the priests, elders, and scribes wanted to get rid of Jesus! He attacked them in the name of the God whose law they claimed to follow to the letter!

They charged Jesus with plotting to destroy the temple, their seat of worship. And they charged him with usurping the authority of God. "Are you the Messiah, the son of the Blessed One?" the high priest asked him. Jesus answered simply, "I am." The high priest tore his clothes and said, "Why do we still need witnesses? You have heard his blasphemy! What is your decision?" They all condemned Jesus and declared that he deserved to die. "Some began to spit on him, to blindfold him, and to strike him, saying to him, 'Prophesy!'" (Mark 14:60–65).

Jesus was a thorn in the side of the religious authorities because he challenged their claim to moral superiority. They felt justified in getting rid of him. They did it in the name of righteousness.

Some of the worst atrocities in human history have been committed in the name of religion, from the justification of the institution of slavery, to ethnic cleansing in Bosnia, to the assassination of Yitzhak Rabin. In personal relationships, "moral superiority" can become a "reason" for excluding and hurting others, and it can blind us to the real needs and circumstances of another person.

In the name of righteousness, the religious authorities bound Jesus, led him away, and handed him over to Pilate, the Roman governor of Judea. Were you there with them?

Pilate

As Jesus stood before Pilate, the charges shifted from religious to political, from blasphemy to treason, and the underlying issue shifted from moral superiority to power. As the Roman procurator, Pilate was the governor of the district that included Judea, Samaria, and Idumea. The power of the absent emperor was his. As a relatively new governor, Pilate feared anyone who might threaten his absolute control of the territory. He didn't worry about priests, elders, and scribes; their authority was limited to matters of religion and day-to-day life. But someone who claimed to be a king was another matter. Was Jesus a revolutionary who might lead an insurrection against the Roman emperor? Such a person could indeed be a threat to the power of the governor of Judea.

We condemn Pilate, yet we may be able to understand how he felt. How are our own lives governed by the desire for power, position, and status? What would we do to climb the ladder of success? How willing are we to stand up for what we believe if it might cost a promotion or our popularity? How do we react when our authority is questioned, on the job and in our homes? How is power a factor in the "isms" in our society—racism, sexism, militarism, materialism?

Pilate saw in Jesus a possible threat to his power. "Are you the King of the Jews?" he asked. According to Mark, Jesus replied only, "You say so" (15:2). Jesus' silence and his calm in the presence of his accusers caused Pilate to "wonder." The man standing before him did not seem dangerous. Pilate was inclined to let him go. But he also worried about another threat to his power: he feared public opinion.

Members of the crowd came to Pilate and asked him to release a prisoner for them, a custom that Mark says was traditional during the celebration of Passover. Perhaps Pilate's greatest sin was refusing to accept the responsibility that was clearly his. He turned his decision over to the crowd. "Do you want me to release for you the King of the Jews?" he asked them (15:9).

We can imagine the defensive thoughts that ran through his mind—and they sound familiar to us. "It isn't my fault." "I'm not responsible; they've taken the matter out of my hands." "I really don't have a choice."

Trying to escape the responsibility for a difficult decision, Pilate turned the fate of Jesus over to the crowd. Were you there with Pilate?

The Crowd

At this point, the bystanders, who had gathered out of curiosity, became participants in the story. The chief priests agitated for the release of a prisoner named Barabbas. Pilate asked the crowd again, "What do you wish me to do with the man you call the King of the Jews?" The crowd shouted back, "Crucify him!" Pilate asked them, "Why, what evil has he done?" But they shouted all the more, "Crucify him!" (Mark 15:12–13).

The religious and Roman authorities had a clear motive to get rid of Jesus. The members of the crowd, however, were merely followers. Blindly, they parroted the strongest voices. Mindlessly, they went along with the passions of the mob. Psychologists tell us that groups will do things that most of the individuals within the group wouldn't do on their own. Some extreme examples are mass suicides committed by cult members and gang rapes conducted before cheering onlookers. To follow the crowd is easy; to stand up against it is hard. To listen with silent assent to a racist joke or a sexist slur is easy; to speak out is difficult.

Politicians well understand mass psychology. The first goal of a campaign is momentum, for they know that if their candidate wins the early races, people will quickly jump on the bandwagon.

They "stir up the crowd" with negative campaigning and sound bites that virtually squeeze all substance out of the debate.

Advertisers, too, know how to stir up the crowd. With subtle and not-so-subtle innuendos, they suggest that a fulfilling love life, a successful career, and the stamp of social approval go to those who drink the right beverage or use the right toothpaste. To sell their products, they stir up the crowd by sponsoring TV programs that cater to the public's lust for violence. An increasing volume of data indicates that violence on TV stirs up the violence in our society.

Bombarded from all directions by voices that stir up the crowd, each person must decide, "Whom shall I follow? Shall I follow the loudest voice? How can I sort out the voices? How do I know the difference between false prophets and true prophets? How can I quiet the roar of the crowd and tune in to the stillness of the Spirit of Christ within? How can I gain the courage to follow Christ when voices around me shout 'Crucify him'"?

The priests, elders, and scribes stirred up the crowd, and the crowd responded to their voices. Were you there in the crowd?

The Cross

Roman soldiers mocked Jesus and led him to Golgotha, also called Calvary.[3] At nine o'clock in the morning, they nailed Jesus to the cross. With him, they crucified two bandits, one on the right and one on the left. Jesus' earthly journey, the way to Jerusalem and the cross, had ended.

Jesus could have chosen another way. He had other options. One was to give in to selfishness, greed, envy, and lust for power. That option would have meant joining God's enemies, or even refusing to acknowledge that God has enemies. An opposite choice was the path of the zealots, the road of violence, fighting evil with more evil, returning hatred with more hatred. Jesus refused both of these options. He chose the way of the cross. He named as enemies those whose ways were contrary to God's ways, and he resisted them with unflinching courage. At the same time, he rejected the way of violence. He absorbed the hatred that was directed at him and returned it with love. He broke the vicious cycle of anger and retaliation. He refused to let himself be defined by evil.

Jesus chose instead the way of suffering. And he taught his followers that to *see* properly, to truly acknowledge Jesus as the Christ, is to recognize the way of the cross and to follow him in that way. There are no easy paths to discipleship. But bearing and sharing the suffering of others is the ultimate act of love.

Were you there with Jesus on the cross?

At first glance, the question seems presumptuous, almost blasphemous. Of course, we were not there on the cross with Jesus! Jesus' self-sacrificing act of love was unique. No other human action can compare to it.

Yet in a sense, all Christians were there with Jesus. Jesus had said to his disciples, "If any want to become my followers, let them deny themselves and take up their cross and follow me" (Mark 8:34). Later he said to James and John, "The cup that I drink, you will drink; and with the baptism with which I am baptized, you will be baptized" (Mark 10:39). By "cup" and "baptism" he meant death on the cross. In a very real way, the cross is part of the job description of every Christian.

Jesus included his followers in his act of sacrifice when he broke bread and said, "Take, this is my body." He joined them to himself when he offered them a cup and said, "This is my blood of the covenant, which is poured out for many" (Mark 14:22–24). Later, the apostle Paul would say it in these words: "All of us who have been baptized into Christ Jesus were baptized into his death" (Rom. 6:3).

Yes, you were there with Jesus on the cross.

The Centurion

From noon until three o'clock, deep clouds covered the sun. Then Jesus cried out in a loud voice, uttering the first words of Psalm 22, "My God, my God, why have you forsaken me?" Soon after that, he gave another loud cry and breathed his last.

A centurion who witnessed this scene said, "Truly this man was God's son" (Mark 15:39). The centurion was a Roman soldier, the commander of the execution squad. Probably he had been in charge of the prisoner since the time of his trial before Pilate. He would have seen the quiet courage with which Jesus faced the Roman governor. He would have watched the soldiers mock him. Perhaps he even participated when the soldiers clothed Jesus in a purple cloak, twisted some thorns into a crown, and placed it on his head. He may have been among the soldiers who saluted Jesus and shouted mockingly, "Hail, King of the Jews!" He would have observed Jesus' unruffled calm as the soldiers spit on him and knelt down in mocking homage. He would have stood before the cross and watched Jesus suffer. He would have shared the hours of waiting for the end to come. Now this Roman soldier, an outsider to Judaism, spoke in words that held no mockery, "Truly this man was God's son."

Mark's witness to Jesus as the Messiah, the Christ, and the Son of God comes to a climax in these words. Mark has been leading up to this proclamation throughout his whole Gospel. Before Jesus had embarked on the journey to Jerusalem, he had asked Peter, "Who do you say that I am?" Peter had answered, "You are the Messiah." As we saw in chapter 1, Jesus' response was surprising. He did not commend Peter for his clear perception, but instead ordered his disciples not to tell anyone about him. He knew they did not understand what it meant to be the Messiah or to be a follower of God's Christ. He began to teach them that the Messiah must undergo great suffering and be rejected and killed and after three days rise again (8:29–31). In Mark, the title of *Christ* cannot be understood outside of the context of the cross.

By the time the high priest questioned Jesus, the cross was clearly in sight. There was no longer any possibility that his followers would misunderstand the meaning of his claim. Therefore, when the high priest asked, "Are you the Messiah?" Jesus answered plainly, "I am."

Jesus' enemies did not understand his statement. Yet in their mockery they conferred on him the title "King of the Jews."

Mark's readers would have understood this title to mean the Messiah, God's anointed one. After Pilate handed Jesus over to be crucified, the soldiers mocked him as a king, bowing down to him and crowning him with thorns. When he was crucified, the inscription of the charge against him read, "King of the Jews." The chief priests and scribes also mocked him, saying, "Let the Messiah, the King of Israel, come down from the cross now" (Mark 15:32).

Lamar Williamson explains that up to this point, Mark has presented Jesus as the Messiah, the King of the Jews, and the Son of God, but his coronation is ironic. "His throne is a cross, his courtiers two robbers, and his public the enemies who kill him."[4]

After Jesus died, a Roman soldier finally recognized the truth. This outsider to Judaism was the first to proclaim the title without misunderstanding and without irony. He said, "Truly this man was God's son." In Williamson's words, Mark's Gospel "points to Jesus on the cross and says, 'God is like that.'"[5]

The Roman centurion was healed of his blindness. Were you there with him?

Joseph of Arimathea

On Friday evening, after Jesus had breathed his last, a new figure entered the story. He is Joseph of Arimathea, a respected member of the Jewish council. All the members of this council had earlier condemned Jesus to death (Mark 14:64). In this former enemy of Jesus, Mark shows us another person whose blindness was healed by witnessing Jesus' death on the cross.

Although he had been one of those who condemned Jesus to die, Joseph was seeking the dominion of God, and he waited expectantly for it. There was a quality of openness in this man, a capacity to be changed by the events he had witnessed. Now he looked at the body of Jesus, hanging on the cross. He looked around at those who had gathered to watch and saw no one who might provide a proper burial. The disciples, who normally would have been expected to perform this service, were nowhere to be found. In an act of compassion, Joseph went to Pilate and asked for the body of Jesus. What courage it must have taken to risk the certain disapproval of his peers on the council! He brought a linen cloth, took down the body of Jesus, wrapped it, and laid the body in a tomb that had been hewn out of rock. Then he rolled a stone to seal the entrance.

In the panoramic sweep of the biblical story, Joseph of Arimathea has a "bit part." He enters the story abruptly, and a few sentences later he is gone, never to reappear.[6] Yet in his brief appearance, Mark has given us a hint of the possibility of change, transformation, and newness of life.

Joseph of Arimathea had a change of heart. Were you there with him?

The Women

Several women also gathered at Calvary on that Friday, looking on from a distance as their leader hung from a cross. Mark names three of them as Mary Magdalene, Mary the mother of James the younger and of Joses, and Salome. The others were anonymous women who, in Mark's words, "provided for [Jesus] when he was in Galilee" (15:41).

From the beginning, women had been some of Jesus' most faithful followers. Often unnamed, they came to Jesus in faith, were healed by that faith, and went out to preach to others. Now they followed him to the cross. While the twelve disciples had scattered and fled, these women remained with Jesus to the end. They watched Joseph of Arimathea take Jesus' body down from the cross. The two Marys followed when Joseph laid Jesus' body in the tomb, and they saw where the body was laid.

We sense the faithfulness of these women. They did not betray or deny or run away. As they had been witnesses to the life of Jesus, now they witnessed his death and his burial.

We also sense their fear. They remained at a distance. They took no action. They simply watched and wept.

Were you there, watching and weeping with them?

Living the Story

1. Using the first person "I," tell the story from the point of view of each of the following participants:

   • A priest, elder, or scribe (Mark 14:53–65)
   • Pilate (15:1–15)
   • A member of the crowd (15:6–15)
   • The centurion (15:16–39)
   • Joseph of Arimathea (15:42–46)
   • One of the women (15:40–47)

   Pretend that you are telling the story to someone who has never heard it before. Tell how you felt and why you did what you did. Putting yourself into the circumstances and emotions of that character, tell the story aloud, or write it as a monologue. Pause after you tell each person's story and ask yourself, "How do I see myself in this story?"

2. After reflecting on the ways you see yourself in the story, write a prayer expressing some of your feelings.

3. How were you with Jesus as he died on the cross?

4. Christians today can easily lose sight of the scandalous nature of the cross, which is an instrument of execution. How is the cross a symbol of your faith?

5. Read Psalm 22. Jesus surely was very familiar with the whole psalm. What thoughts and feelings do you think he had as he cried out the first line of this psalm from the cross?

6. Respond to the story through an artistic medium such as charcoal, crayons, pencil, pen, clay, or paint. Let your imagination run free. Don't work toward creating something that someone else might recognize and understand. Just put the chalk, paint, or glob of clay in your hand and see what comes forth. A splash of color, the absence of color, a pounded or broken piece of clay, or the abstract use of line and space can give expression to your emotions. If possible, talk about this experience with someone who is close to you.

7. Meditate on "The Song of the Suffering Servant" (Isa. 53:4–6). Read each line very slowly, reflecting on the way these words,

written six centuries before Jesus was born, speak to you as you reflect on the crucifixion of Jesus. When you come to a line that seems particularly important, close your eyes and repeat it slowly for several minutes.

Surely he has born our infirmities and carried our diseases;
yet we accounted him stricken,
   struck down by God, and afflicted.
But he was wounded for our transgressions,
   crushed for our iniquities;
upon him was the punishment that made us whole,
   and by his bruises we are healed.
All we like sheep have gone astray;
   we have all turned to our own way,
and God has laid on him
   the iniquity of us all.

This Week

Every day, offer a prayer of thanksgiving for Christ's gift of his life.

7

"Their Eyes Were Opened"

Coming to the Story

1. Recall a time when you have been awake in the wee hours of the morning struggling with a painful memory, a temptation, a sense of guilt, or a regret.
2. Read about the events that took place in the wee hours of the morning on the third day after Jesus was crucified (Mark 16:1–8). Then read three stories of the appearance of the risen Christ: John 20:11–18; Luke 24:13–35; John 21:4–19.
3. Where do you see yourself in these stories?

Reflecting on the Story

Whenever I am in emotional pain, the time I dread most is three o'clock in the morning. Wide awake, I toss and turn—alone, re-membering, wishing. I begin the "if only" syndrome. "If only I had done something different while I had the chance." I struggle to think of something—anything—I could yet do to make things different.

Is this the way Mary Magdalene felt in the hours before dawn on the first Easter morning? Did she think, "If only I had done something different while I had the chance"? And then did an idea suddenly strike her; did she think of something she could yet do? Her idea to visit the tomb of Jesus is the kind of ill-conceived idea that sometimes takes shape in the wee hours of the morning. Not until they were on their way did it occur to the two Marys and Salome that they might have a problem. They had watched Joseph of Arimathea roll a stone over the entrance to the tomb. "Who will roll the stone away?" they said to one another (Mark 16:1–3).

Much to their amazement, they arrived to find the stone rolled back! When they entered the tomb, a young man dressed in a white robe delivered a message straight from God: "He has been raised; he is not here! . . . Go, tell the disciples and Peter that he is going ahead of you to Galilee; there you will see him, just as he told you." The women ran from the tomb, grasped by amazement and fear (Mark 16:4–8).

This is the end of Mark's Gospel, according to the earliest and most authentic manuscripts. Some translations include a shorter or a longer ending, but most biblical scholars agree that both of these endings were written more than a century later. Mark ends with the words, "They said nothing to anyone, for they were afraid" (Mark 16:8). Mark does not tell us that the women eventually followed the angel's command to "Go tell." He does not report any appearances of the risen Christ.

The abruptness of Mark's ending startles us. Some translators have noted that it seems to be cut off in mid-sentence. They have suggested that the last sentence should be translated, "They said nothing to anyone, for they were afraid of . . ."[1] Was Mark interrupted in his writing? Was a piece of the manuscript lost? Or did Mark deliberately end his Gospel abruptly? Scholars have argued all sides of this question, and we can't be certain of the answer. But many students of the Bible think that Mark wrote the ending exactly as we have it, with intentional abruptness.

Why would Mark leave his story unfinished?

Mark must have known at least some of the stories of the Resurrection that are included in the other Gospels. His whole Gospel, the "Good News of Jesus Christ," is predicated on this knowledge. Mark knew that the disciples saw Jesus again after he had been crucified and buried. He knew the Easter experience freed them from their fear, gave them voice to "go and tell," and transformed their lives. Mark knew that when the disciples encountered the risen Christ, they were healed of the blindness that he had portrayed so painfully throughout his Gospel. Why would Mark leave his story unfinished?

We will return to this question. For the moment, however, let's turn to the other Gospels to see some of the stories Mark did not include. Let's consider these early testimonies of resurrection faith and see how the disciples' blindness was healed.

Recognition

In several of the Easter stories, Jesus appeared to his followers, but they didn't recognize him! Luke tells of two disciples walking toward the village of Emmaus late on Easter day. One was named Cleopas. The other is not named. (I like to think it was Mrs. Cleopas.) As they walked, a "stranger" joined them. They poured out their hearts to him, telling him about Jesus whom they had thought to be the Messiah and about the Crucifixion that had crushed their hopes. In bewilderment, they told him of rumors that Jesus had been seen, alive again. The "stranger" talked with them about the meaning of all these events, interpreting them in the light of Hebrew prophecy. When they reached the village, he turned to leave, but Cleopas persuaded him to stay and eat with them. At last, in the breaking of the bread, their eyes were opened and they recognized the stranger as Jesus, the Christ (Luke 24:13–32).

In John's account of the empty tomb, we notice the same initial lack of recognition. Mary had gone to the tomb and found it empty. She saw a man she assumed to be the gardener. Even when he spoke to her, she didn't recognize him. In her agitation and fear she said, "Sir, if you have carried him away, tell me where you have laid him, and I will take him away." Finally, he said, "Mary!" Hearing him call her by name, she recognized him at last. "Rabbouni!" she said, meaning "teacher" (John 20:11–18).

In John 21, Jesus appeared to his disciples on the beach while they were fishing. Again, they did not know who he was. Only after he directed them to cast their net on the other side and they brought in a tremendous catch of fish did they recognize him (vv. 4–19).

In Matthew, the eleven disciples had gone to Galilee as Jesus had directed them. The issue of the recognition of the Christ is given in one simple sentence: "When they saw him, they worshiped him; but some doubted" (28:16–17).

We may experience Christ in the breaking of bread as Cleopas did, by hearing a voice call our name as Mary did, or by sensing a command to change what we are doing as the disciples did. Always, recognition of the living Christ comes from the perspective of faith.

When have you recognized the presence of Christ in your life? At a hospital bedside? In the face of a child? In the touch of a friend? Looking back, how do you believe that Christ was present, even in ways you may have overlooked at the time?

A member of our congregation stood up one day and told how she had recognized the presence of Christ in the breaking of bread. Their son—I'll call him Craig—had been in a drug treatment program. While he was in the program, his parents served dinner every Wednesday night to a group of teenaged substance abusers. Members of our congregation furnished these meals, week after week, for nearly a year. After Craig graduated from the program, his mother told the congregation, "Those meals were a minicommunion service every Wednesday. Christ was truly present, breaking bread with us, in every one of the meals you provided." From the perspective of faith, we recognize the presence of the living Christ in our lives.

Reconciliation

How might the disciples have felt when they recognized the resurrected Jesus? Amazed, bewildered, and frightened? Yes. Joyful? Certainly. And surely one of their feelings must also have been guilt. Peter had denied him. They all had abandoned him. How could Jesus ever forgive them for betraying, denying, and deserting? How could they forgive themselves? How could they continue to count themselves as Christ's friends?

The issue of forgiveness is central to our understanding of the meaning of Jesus' death and resurrection. Very early, the followers of Christ began to interpret Jesus death' in terms of redemption. Jesus had addressed the need for forgiveness in the last meal that he shared with his disciples, as we saw in chapter 4. He told them they would betray, deny, and fall away, but they didn't believe him. Because they didn't see themselves as sinners, they could not receive the gift of grace Jesus offered them. Throughout the Gospel stories, the people who are most able to respond to Jesus are those who recognize themselves as forgiven sinners. The prodigal son, the woman who bathed Jesus' feet with her tears, Zacchaeus, and the tax collector who prayed "God, have mercy on me a sinner" are but a few examples.[2] The disciples had failed to acknowledge that they were sinners.

After Good Friday, the situation was entirely different. The disciples saw themselves as they were, and they didn't like what they saw. Their relationship with Jesus was broken, and they had broken it. How could they now face Jesus? How could their relationship be restored?

The disciples could not bring reconciliation, but they didn't have to. Jesus did it for them.

After the Resurrection, Jesus continued to do what he had always done. He drew his followers into close relationship. He called them by name. He walked and talked with them. He broke bread with them.

Perhaps the most poignant story of reconciliation is Jesus' conversation with Peter on the shore of the Sea of Galilee in John 21 after Jesus appeared to the disciples while they were fishing. In a scene reminiscent of their last supper, Jesus took bread and gave it to them. Then he asked Peter, "Do you love me?" Peter answered, "Yes. You know I love you." Three times, Jesus asked the same question, "Do you love me?" Each time Peter gave the same answer, "You know I love you." Jesus did not ask the question to test Peter's love. Jesus knew Peter loved him. He asked the question for Peter's sake. Three times, Jesus gave him the opportunity to express the love he had denied three times.

Near the end of the movie *Terms of Endearment*, a young son stands at the bedside of his dying mother. Immature and unwilling to face the reality of her death, he snaps at her because she suggests that he cut his hair. He is unable to utter the words of love his mother knows he will someday wish he had said. With a mother's insight and understanding she assures him, "I know that you love me."

By the Sea of Galilee, the risen Christ gave Peter the chance to say what he had been unable to say in the courtyard of the high priest: "You know I love you." As he had in the upper room, Jesus responded to human failure by continuing to draw the sinner into closer relationship. It was an act of reconciliation and forgiveness.

Forgiveness does not mean saying, "Oh, that's all right." Betrayal, denial, and desertion are not okay. Dishonesty, destructiveness, and selfishness are not okay. Forgiveness does not make them okay.

Forgiveness means putting the past where it belongs—in the past. It lets past mistakes be *over*—not okay, but over, so that mistakes of the past do not continue to work their destruction in the present and the future. Forgiveness offers a new beginning, new hope, a new day, a new song, and new life.

Nothing is more difficult for human beings than to forgive. Changing our feelings isn't an act we can do on command, and unconfronted anger has a way of continuing to work its corrosive power in our lives. A friend of mine struggled to forgive her mother, with whom she had ample reason to be angry. Her sister often lectured her about trying to forgive, but all the lectures accomplished was to make her angry at her sister! She did not make progress toward reconciliation until a competent counselor helped her discover that some seeds of forgiveness had already begun to grow in her mind and spirit.

The good news of Easter is that between us and God, forgiveness has already happened. Christ has already done the work of reconciliation. Christ simply asks us, "Do you love me?" And he already knows the answer. Forgiveness may come more slowly in our human relationships, but when we learn to recognize ourselves as sinners whom God has forgiven, we begin to discover our ability to forgive ourselves and one another.

Transformation

Forgiveness is a free gift, but its purpose is not just to give us the warm, fuzzy feeling that we are okay. Grace is not about warm, fuzzy feelings. It is about the restoration of relationship with God. That relationship transforms our lives.

In several of the resurrection stories, the way Jesus communicated reconciliation and forgiveness to his followers was by giving them a renewed mission. In John 21, after Peter told Jesus, "You know I love you," Jesus asked something of Peter: "Feed my lambs." Friendship with Christ moves us outward. The assignment of a mission is, in fact, an integral part of grace.

I can relate to this story. One time when my husband and I were struggling with a particularly difficult issue, I was having a hard time both forgiving and feeling forgiven. Three words broke the struggle loose for me. He said simply, "I need you." To feel needed is a fundamental part of feeling accepted.

In several of the resurrection stories, the risen Christ told his disciples, in effect, "I need you." He commanded the women at the empty tomb to go tell the disciples what they had seen (Matt. 28:10; John 20:17).[3] In Luke, Jesus instructed his followers to proclaim repentance and forgiveness of sins in his name "to all nations, beginning from Jerusalem" (24:45–49). In Matthew, Jesus said, "Go therefore and make disciples of all nations, baptizing them . . . and teaching them to obey everything that I have commanded you" (28:16–20). In John, Jesus stood among the disciples who were gathered in the upper room and said, "As [God] has sent me, so I send you" (20:21).

By the power of his reconciling love, the living Christ continues to draw us into close relationship. He makes us partners in his continuing mission in the world. And our lives are transformed! The leaders of the early church, particularly the apostle Paul, struggled to find words to express this transforming relationship. We are "the body of Christ." We are "members of Christ." We have "the mind of Christ." We are "in Christ." Christ "lives in us." We have "clothed [ourselves] with Christ." We have become "partners of Christ."[4] In close relationship with Christ, we begin to see the world through Christ's eyes.

For the followers of Jesus who experienced the presence of the living Christ, nothing could ever be the same. Suddenly they saw themselves differently. They began to break free of the bonds of weakness, fear, and sin that had held them. They began to feel Christ's power within them. They saw others differently, too. They caught a glimpse of Christ's vision of a world governed by justice and love. They began reaching out to others in brand new ways. In the story of the early church, we see the dramatic change that took place in the lives of the disciples.

Look at Peter. Peter had tried to persuade Jesus not to make the journey to the cross and had consistently turned blind eyes to the idea of a messiah who must suffer and die. In the courtyard of the high priest, Peter had denied Jesus three times. After that, he ran away and hid. Then Peter experienced the presence of the risen Christ. And look at the change that occurred! This same Peter stood up on the day of Pentecost and boldly proclaimed the message of the risen Christ, urging people to believe and be baptized. Day after day, this same Peter went out with John on the streets of Jerusalem preaching the gospel. One time he was arrested, and his captors offered to release him if he would promise not to teach or preach in the name of Jesus. And Peter, the same Peter who had once denied his Christ, looked at his captors and said calmly, "We cannot keep from speaking about what we have seen and heard" (Acts 4:1–20). According to tradition, Peter eventually made his way to Rome where he was martyred for his beliefs.

Look at the change that took place in the other disciples! Before the Resurrection, we saw them arguing about who was the greatest (Mark 9:34). James and John wanted to sit on Jesus' right and left hand in his glory (Mark 10:37). The disciples criticized the woman at Bethany for anointing Jesus' body with expensive perfume, an act that Jesus called "good" or "beautiful." When Jesus asked them to watch with him in the Garden of Gethsemane, they fell asleep. They protested that they would never desert Jesus, but when he was arrested, tried, and crucified, the disciples disappeared.

Then Easter dawned! Suddenly the disciples came out of hiding. Like Peter, they began preaching on the streets of Jerusalem. Like Peter, they were arrested and flogged (Acts 5:18, 40). James was killed with a sword (Acts 12:2). But the disciples faced death without fear. "Every day in the temple and at home, they did not cease to teach and proclaim Jesus as the Messiah" (Acts 5:42). John Shelby Spong, in *The Easter Moment*, describes their transition from cowards into heroes:

> They launched a mission and a movement that literally exploded onto the stage of human history. It created a new holy day. It broke out of the limitation of Jewish nationalism into a universalism. It conquered the civilized Western world in less than 300 years. . . . Something happened in the Moment of Easter that created enormous changes and ignited enormous power.[5]

What happened to Peter? What happened to the other disciples? What changed fleeing cowards into courageous heros?

What happened was the Resurrection! The disciples experienced the risen Christ. They experienced the power of God's reconciling love.

The journey through Good Friday to Easter healed the blindness of Jesus' followers. The stories of the disciples' response to the risen Christ demonstrate the change that took place.

Why didn't Mark include these stories? We return now to the question raised at the beginning of the chapter. Why would Mark end his Gospel with the words, "[The women] said nothing to anyone, for they were afraid"? Why would Mark, who so painstakingly portrayed the blindness of Jesus' followers, fail to include accounts of their healing? Why would Mark leave his story unfinished?

Mark's unfinished ending emphasizes the unfinished nature of the story itself.[6] Mark knew that Jesus appeared to his disciples, both men and women, after he had been crucified and buried. But that wasn't the end of the story.

Mark knew that the disciples' eyes were opened and they recognized the risen Christ. But that wasn't the end of the story either.

Mark knew that the disciples' eyes were opened and they saw themselves as forgiven sinners, Christ's friends, messengers, and partners. But that wasn't the end of the story.

Mark knew that the disciples' eyes were opened and they beheld Christ's vision for the world. They understood at last that to live toward that vision meant to follow Christ in the way of self-sacrificing love. Even that was not the end of the story.

The end of the story must be written in the heart and mind of every reader. Mark has given us his Gospel about Jesus the Christ who lived a life of self-sacrificing love, died on a cross for our sake, lives again, and continues to call us to follow him. Mark shouts out the proclamation of the angel who guarded the empty tomb: "He is going ahead of you. . . . You will see him just as he told you" (16:7).

As we conclude our journey to the cross, Mark leaves us with a question: "Here is the good news," he says. "Can you *see?*"

Living the Story

1. What might have prevented Jesus' followers from recognizing him? What prevents us from recognizing Christ's presence in our lives?

2. At the village of Emmaus, why might the moment of recognition have come in the breaking of the bread? How have you felt Christ's presence in the breaking of bread?

3. How might hearing Jesus call her name have helped Mary recognize him? How is Christ calling your name?

4. How did Jesus' suggestion to the disciples, "Cast your net on the other side," help them recognize him? How is Christ suggesting a change in your life?

5. How do you think Peter felt when Jesus asked him, "Do you love me?"

6. How have you experienced God's grace in the past? How is God offering you the gift of grace right now?

7. The apostle Paul said, "Christ lives in me." Write a letter to yourself from Jesus describing how Jesus sees you. Include observations of ways Christ lives in you.

8. How do you think Peter felt when Jesus said, "Feed my lambs"? How is mission a part of grace? How is Christ saying to you, "I need you?"

9. The apostle Paul and other writers of the early church expressed their continuing relationship with Christ in a variety of images. Choose one of the following images and express it in a drawing, a poem, a song, a dance, a brief essay, or a prayer:

   • We are the "body of Christ" (1 Cor. 12:27).
   • We are "members of Christ" (1 Cor. 6:15).
   • We have "the mind of Christ" (1 Cor. 2:16).
   • We are "in Christ" (Rom. 8:1).
   • Christ "lives in me" (Gal. 2:20).
   • We have "clothed [ourselves] with Christ" (Gal. 3:27).
   • We are "partners of Christ" (Hebrews 3:14).

10. Meditate on a key phrase from the Easter story. Following are some suggestions. Repeat the phrase slowly or picture yourself in the scene.

   • "You will see him" (Mark 16:7).
   • "Stay with us" (Luke 24:29).
   • "Their eyes were opened" (Luke 24:31).
   • Jesus said, "*(use your own name)* " (John 20:16).
   • "I have seen the Lord" (John 20:18).
   • "Do you love me?" (John 21:15–17).
   • "Feed my lambs" (John 21:15).

This Week

Celebrate your transforming friendship with the living Christ! Write God a thank-you note; give flowers to a friend or to an enemy; plant a daffodil or a tree; watch a sunrise; hang a joyful symbol in your window or on your wall; put balloons on your mailbox or your door; eat cookies with someone who will rejoice with you; or find some other exuberant way to celebrate.

Guide for Group Study

Spiritual growth happens best in community, and *Journey to the Cross* lends itself to group study, particularly in the season of Lent. This section provides some suggestions for using this book with a group.

Underlying Assumptions

1. The Bible is central to the group's study. Read or tell the story directly from the Bible as part of each session.
2. Where two or more are gathered in Christ's name, Christ's spirit is present with them (Matt. 18:20). The leader's task is simply to help the group gather around the biblical word and to create an environment where that word can speak to their lives. There is no need to attempt to persuade any person to a particular point of view. That is the work of the spirit!
3. Spiritual growth happens best in community; therefore it is important to give attention to the process of building community. Trust in any group is fragile and builds slowly. Structure the sessions so that they move gradually from low-risk interaction to deeper reflection and personal sharing. Arrange the learning area in a way that allows participants to see one another's faces. Set chairs in a circle or in a semicircular arrangement with as many rows as you need to accommodate the group. Or seat the group around a table.

Course Structure

The ideal length of the study is eight meetings, one for each of the seven chapters and an introductory session in which books are

distributed and the course is introduced. The ideal length of time
for each session is one and a half to two hours, but of course, plans
can be adapted to the length of time you have available.

Each session might include the following: (1) opening prayer,
(2) coming to the story, (3) reading the story, (4) reflecting on the
story, (5) closing.

The Introductory Session

The first meeting can follow the pattern outlined above, but it
will be somewhat different from the other seven sessions because
the group members will not have begun to read the book. The introductory session needs to introduce the course and to begin
building a sense of community.

First, open with prayer.

Next, prepare to come to the story. In the introductory session,
the time allotted to "Coming to the Story" should be much longer
than it will be in the other sessions. Begin with an introductory
activity such as this one: Ask the participants to pair up with
someone with whom they are not well acquainted and find out
the following information about that person: name; three things
they didn't know about that person; one hope he or she has for
this study group. Allow five to eight minutes for interviews. Then
have the partners introduce each other to the group.

The introductory session is also a good time to make a group
covenant. Print the following guidelines on newsprint and ask the
group to suggest additions or changes:

• Share time equally.
• Keep confidentiality.
• Speak for yourself only.
    • Make "I" statements.
    • Avoid giving advice.
• Value everyone's opinions.
• Respect another person's right to remain silent.

Next, read the story in Mark 8:27–35 in one of the ways described in "Reading the Story" below. Reading and discussing this

text will serve as a good introduction to chapter 1, which will be the reading assignment for the second session.

Then reflect on the story. Ask questions to draw out the meaning of the biblical story. Avoid right/wrong questions like "What did Jesus ask Peter?" Frame your questions in ways that allow more than one "right" answer and that encourage the expression of different points of view. "Jesus did not congratulate Peter for recognizing him as the Messiah; why do you think he didn't?" "Why do you think Jesus spoke so sharply to Peter?" "What does this section of Mark show us about the Messiah?" In the introductory session, the primary purpose of the reflection on the scripture is to spark the learners' curiosity about the text rather than to draw conclusions. They will read and reflect on an interpretation of this scripture in chapter 1.

Assign chapter 1 for the next session. If you decide to make a standard assignment for each session as described under "Reflecting on the Story, Option 1" below, explain that assignment. Close with prayer.

After the introductory meeting, the group members will have had the opportunity to read and reflect on the assigned chapter. The flow of the sessions will be different, but each session will follow the five-part pattern outlined above. Specific suggestions for each of the five parts follow.

Opening Prayer

Open with prayer asking God to guide and inspire this time of reflection and to open each heart to the presence of God's spirit.

Coming to the Story

Take ten to fifteen minutes at the beginning of each session to build community and to lead into the biblical story. Think of this time as warm-up or breaking the ice, a time to help people interact in ways that are easy, entertaining, and low risk. A good place to find ideas for this warmup is in the first item in "Coming to the Story" in each chapter. Restate the question to encourage

short answers. For example, in chapter 4, "Coming to the Story,"
no. 1, states: "Recall some of the times in your life when you have
gathered at a table with people you love. . . . How have these
times of sharing food and companionship influenced your life?"
To frame the question in a way that elicits short answers, you
might say something like this: "Recall a time when you have sat
at a table with people you love. [Pause] What are some of the feelings you had as you sat at these tables?" The answers might include "happy, comfortable, welcome, accepted as I am." Often it
works well to list the answers, without discussion, in single
words or short phrases on newsprint.

Reading the Story

Reading the biblical story as a group makes it fresh in everyone's
minds. "Coming to the Story," no. 2, gives the scripture refer-
ences for each chapter. Read or tell the story in new and interesting ways. Vary the method. Avoid the common practice of having each person read a verse. Here are some possibilities:

- Act out the story. Assign key roles to volunteers. Try to make
  everyone a participant by including them as "onlookers" or
  "the crowd."
- Have a good reader read the story aloud while the others listen
  with eyes closed.
- Tell the story from the point view of persons who were there.
  Divide into small groups, assign each group a character, and
  have them read the story, talk about it, and select a volunteer
  to tell the story to the larger group using the first person "I."
- Tell the story as a group. Divide into small groups and assign
  each group a part of the story. As above, have the groups talk
  among themselves and then select a volunteer to tell their part
  of the story to the whole group.
- Imagine yourself in the story. Have the group members close
  their eyes as you tell the story from a "You Are There" point of
  view. "Reflecting on the Story," chapters 2 and 4, contain examples of this kind of imagining.

Reflecting on the Story

If your group is larger than seven, reflect on the story in groups of four to seven. This reflection may be handled in one of two ways, as outlined below.

Option 1. At the introductory meeting, make the following standard assignment for each of the other sessions: "Read the whole chapter, including 'Coming to the Story,' the biblical story itself, 'Reflecting on the Story,' and the questions and exercises that follow in 'Living the Story.' For each chapter, choose a question or exercise that seems particularly important to you, and be prepared to share with your small group something about your reflection on it."

At the second meeting, establish small groups that will remain together throughout all the sessions. In these groups, all members are invited to tell their group something about their reflection on the question they chose, while the others listen without extensive discussion and without trying to solve any of the issues that are raised. Before the second session, give careful consideration to the makeup of these groups. Separate spouses and close friends, people who are extra-talkative, and people who are extra-quiet. Appoint a facilitator for each group, choosing someone who can monitor the time tactfully to ensure that each person has an opportunity to speak.

Option 2. Choose a few of the questions and exercises from "Living the Story" for reflection in groups of four to seven. Ahead of time, print these questions on newsprint or on a sheet or card for each group.

"Reflecting on the Story" contains two types of questions. Some call for interpretation of the scripture, such as, "What gave Jesus the strength to choose the way that led to Jerusalem and the cross?" (chapter 1, "Living," no. 4). Questions of interpretation can be discussed by the small group as a whole. Other questions call for personal application of the Bible story, such as, "What hard choice do you see in your life right now? What might Jesus say to you about this choice?" (chapter 1, "Living," no. 6).

Living the story and taking its meaning for our own lives is the ultimate objective of all Bible study. Personal questions, however, should be handled very carefully. Such sharing must be voluntary. Never try to force it. Avoid putting anyone on the spot. Offer a variety of options, both in the choice of questions or exercises and in the manner of sharing the experience with others. In chapter 3, for example, you might have the participants choose between "Living," no. 6, writing a dialogue, or no. 7, writing a prayer of confession. When they have finished, invite volunteers (only those who wish to) to read their dialogue to the group, choosing a partner to help them read. Invite those who wrote prayers to read a part of them during the closing.

Closing

In the closing, offer the group's experience to God and ask God's continued presence and guidance. Here are some possibilities:

• Pray in your own words.
• Offer a time of silence and an invitation for individual prayers.
• Use scripture or poetry. (The meditation at the end of each chapter's "Living the Story" offers some suggestions.)
• Incorporate some of the group's work, such as prayers written or pictures drawn.
• Sing a favorite Lenten hymn.
• For chapter 4, consider asking a pastor to close with communion.

At the last session, celebrate the presence of the living Christ throughout your time together. Here are two possibilities for this celebration: (1) Tell the group specific ways that you have felt Christ's presence during the time you have been meeting together. For instance, you might say, "I felt Christ's presence when I told you all how worried I was about my mother and Eileen gave me a big hug." Then invite the members of the group to tell about ways they have experienced Christ's presence in the life of the group. (2) Attach yarn or ribbon to pieces of 8½" x 11" poster board so group members can wear them around their necks with the poster board hanging at their backs. Invite all the participants to move around the room and to write on each person's card a way they sense the presence of the living Christ in that person. For example, they might write: "I see Christ in your smile!" or "I felt Christ's love when I told you how rotten I had been acting and you liked me anyway."

May God guide and bless you as you seek to join in community with others on a journey to the cross.

Notes

1. "Teacher, Let Me See!"

1. *The Common Lectionary* was an adaptation of the Roman Catholic lectionary, published in 1969 in response to Vatican II.

2. *Common Lectionary: The Lectionary Proposed by the Consultation on Common Texts* (New York: Church Hymnal Corporation, 1981), 13–14.

3. For the analysis of Mark 8:22–10:52, I am indebted to my remarkable New Testament professor, Dr. Reginald H. Fuller of Virginia Theological Seminary, Alexandria, Virginia. Dr. Fuller credits Alan Richardson, *The Miracle Stories of the Gospels* (London: SCM Press, 1948), and Norman Perrin's essay in *Christology and a Modern Pilgrimage*, ed. Hans-Dieter Betz (Claremont, Calif.: New Testament Colloquium, 1971). A similar interpretation and an excellent discussion of the same subject is found in Lamar Williamson Jr., *Mark: Interpretation—A Bible Commentary for Teaching and Preaching*, ed. James Luther Mays (Louisville: John Knox Press, 1983), 4–5, 147–57, 196–200.

3. "You Will All Fall Away"

1. Jim Wallis, *A Call to Conversion* (San Francisco: Harper & Row, 1981), 49.

2. Luke calls Simon "the zealot." Mark (3:18) and Matthew (10:4) call him "the Cananaean," derived from the Aramaic word *quan'an'*, "zealous." See *Harper's Bible Dictionary*, ed. Paul J. Achtemeier (San Francisco: Harper & Row, 1985), 153.

3. See John 6:15.

4. The prayer is often attributed to the twentieth-century theologian Reinhold Niebuhr, though some claim it dates back to the eighteenth century. It has been used by Alcoholics Anonymous since about 1940.

4. "Do This, Remembering Me"

1. Mark 3:13–19. See also Matt. 10:2–4 and Luke 6:13–16.

2. Williamson (*Mark: Interpretation*, 190) explains that in Greek us-

age, *many* has an inclusive sense, meaning the multitude in contrast to the individual.

3. See Exodus 20:1–3.

4. For some examples, see Ps. 51; Ezek. 18:25–32; Isa. 1:18–20; Lev. 6:1–7, Num. 5:5–7. An excellent discussion of the relationship between repentance and forgiveness in Judaism can be found in L. Gregory Jones, *Embodying Forgiveness* (Grand Rapids, Mich.: Eerdmans, 1995), 107–9.

5. Jones (*Embodying Forgiveness*, 121) emphasizes that Jesus shifts the emphasis from Judaism's assumption that repentance precedes human forgiveness to Christianity's belief that repentance will become an indispensable component of the habit of forgiveness.

5. "Not What I Want, but What You Want"

1. Marcus J. Borg, *Meeting Jesus Again for the First Time* (San Francisco: Harper, 1994), 31–32.

2. Henri J. M. Nouwen, *The Way of the Heart* (New York: Ballantine, 1981), 57–58.

3. Ibid., 65.

4. Ibid., 61.

5. Jer. 49:12; Ezek. 23:31–33; Mark 10:38–39.

6. "Crucify Him!"

1. "Were You There," African American spiritual, *The Hymnal of the UCC* (Philadelphia: United Church Press, 1974), 223.

2. Extensive biblical scholarship has dealt with the discrepancies in the details of the exact time and nature of the trials of Jesus before Jewish and Roman authorities, considering questions such as whether or not the appearance of Jesus before the responsible leaders of his own people was a legally constituted hearing by the Sanhedrin. Williamson (*Mark: Interpretation*, 268) points out that, "We are reading gospel, and the trial narrative should be read as such. This word of caution, particularly apt for Christian attorneys who approach these texts from a legal perspective, calls all interpreters to stress what the text proclaims about Jesus."

3. *Golgotha*, meaning *skull*, is the Hebrew name. *Calvary* derives from the Latin translation of the word.

4. Williamson, *Mark: Interpretation*, 277.

5. Ibid., 278.

6. According to the apocryphal *Gospel of Nicodemus*, Joseph of Arimathea helped to found the first Christian community at Lydda on the coastal plain southwest of Jerusalem.

7. "Their Eyes Were Opened"

1. Frederick C. Grant, *Mark Exegesis* in *The Interpreter's Bible*, vol. 7 (New York: Abingdon-Cokesbury, 1951), 915.

2. See Luke 15:11–32, 7:36–50, 19:1–10, 18:9–14.

3. In Mark and Luke, this command comes from the angels at the tomb.

4. 1 Cor. 12:27, 6:15, 2:16; Rom. 8:1; Gal. 2:20, 3:27; Heb. 3:14.

5. John Shelby Spong, *The Easter Moment* (San Francisco: Harper, 1980), 58.

6. For a good discussion of Mark's unfinished ending, see Williamson, *Mark: Interpretation*, 285–86.

Suggested Reading

Borg, Marcus J. *Meeting Jesus Again for the First Time*. San Francisco: Harper, 1994.

Jones, L. Gregory. *Embodying Forgiveness*. Grand Rapids, Mich.: Eerdmans, 1995.

Nouwen, Henri J. M. *The Way of the Heart*. New York: Ballantine, 1981.

Spong, John Shelby. *The Easter Moment*. San Francisco: Harper, 1980.

Williamson, Lamar, Jr. *Mark: Interpretation—A Bible Commentary for Teaching and Preaching*. Edited by James Luther Mays. Louisville: John Knox Press, 1983.

1912948R0006

Printed in Great Britain
by Amazon.co.uk, Ltd.,
Marston Gate.